Little Wolf
At Leyte

Little Wolf At Leyte

The Story of the Heroic
USS *SAMUEL B. ROBERTS* (DE-413)
in the Battle of Leyte Gulf
During World War II

By

J. HENRY DOSCHER, JR.
Captain USNR (Ret.)

*All royalties from this book will be donated to
Museums of Abilene, Inc.,
Grace Cultural Center, Abilene, Texas.*

Copyright © 1996
By J. Henry Doscher, Jr.

Published in the United States of America
By Eakin Press
An Imprint of Sunbelt Media, Inc.
P.O. Drawer 90159   ★   Austin, TX 78709-0159

ISBN 1-57168-082-9

2   3   4   5   6   7   8   9

Library of Congress Cataloging-in-Publication Data

Doscher, J. Henry
    Little wolf at Leyte : the story of the heroic USS Samuel B. Roberts (DE-413) in the Battle of Leyte Gulf during World War II / by J. Henry Doscher.
        p.   cm.
    Includes bibliographical references (p.   ) and index.
    ISBN 1-57168-082-9
    1. Samuel B. Roberts (Destroyer : DE-413) 2. Philippine Sea, Battles of the, 1944.
3. Leyte Island (Philippines) — History, Military.   I. Title.
D774.S22D67   1996
940.54'25--dc20   96-1398
                                                                                        CIP

This book is dedicated to the memory of

JOHN SCHUMAN LeCLERCQ III
fellow student, fraternity brother, and
fellow officer in the United States Navy,
who gave his life for his country in the
Battle of Leyte Gulf

and

PAUL HENRY CARR
recipient of the Silver Star
who gave his life for his country in the
Battle of Leyte Gulf

and

to all the other officers and men of the
USS *SAMUEL B. ROBERTS*
who so valiantly engaged an overwhelming
Japanese Naval Force off Samar on that fateful morning,
25 October 1944.

In blossom today, then scattered:
Life is so like a delicate flower.
How can one expect the fragrance
To last forever?

> — Personal diary entry by
> Vice Admiral Takijiro Onishi
> Commander, First Air Fleet,
> after ordering the creation of the
> Kamikaze Corps.

See that ye hold fast to the heritage we leave you,
And teach your children its value,
That never in the coming centuries
Their hearts may fail them or their hands grow weak.

> — Inscription on the War Memorial at the
> Royal Naval College in Dartmouth,
> England's Naval Academy.

Contents

Maps

Preface

October 25, 1944! All of us have heard of the Battle of Midway, the bombing of Pearl Harbor, the Normandy landings; yet few Americans know or remember what happened on this historic date. At dawn on this day, off the island of Samar in the extreme western area of the Philippine Sea, another "David vs. Goliath" type of military engagement occurred — a naval battle in which valor, tenacity, and pure old American grit and guts won the day. It was the climactic event of a four-day slugfest known as the Battle of Leyte Gulf; in sum total, the greatest naval battle in the history of the world.

Beginning shortly before midnight on 24 October, and continuing until nearly dawn on 25 October, at Surigao Strait, over 100 miles to the south, Vice Admiral Kinkaid's Seventh Fleet battleships, cruisers and destroyers fought and crushed elements of the Japanese fleet which were attempting to reach our Leyte landings from that direction. That portion of the Battle of Leyte Gulf was between naval forces of similar strength. But at dawn on 25 October, off Samar, the odds were all in favor of the Japanese. Coming from the west out of the San Bernardino Strait and circling around the eastern side of the island of Samar, Vice Admiral Takeo Kurita's mighty force of four battleships, nine heavy cruisers, one light cruiser, and ten destroyers surprised a tiny American force of three destroyers and four destroyer escorts which were acting as an anti-submarine screen for six little "Jeep" carriers. This small American naval unit of Kinkaid's Seventh Fleet was in place off Samar to provide air reconnaissance for General MacArthur's troops, who were fighting at nearby Leyte Island. It was the only American force on the immediate scene after Admiral Halsey, who had been guarding San Bernardino Strait, steamed far to the north with his major ships of the Third Fleet.

Admiral Kurita's force had 6-inch, 8-inch and 18.1-inch guns, the latter the largest in naval history. The small American ships had only 5-inch and even smaller weapons. Comparatively speaking, it was like a pistol vs. a deer rifle!

This book is the story of how an overwhelmed American force turned back the Japanese and thereby saved MacArthur's military landing forces who were fighting at Leyte. That this naval engagement occurred on 25 October is prophetic in itself. More than 500 years earlier, in one of the most remarkable battles in history, King Henry V of England, with a half-starved force, soundly defeated a French army five times larger and much more heavily armed. That was the Battle of Agincourt, 25 October 1415, celebrated by Shakespeare in his play named for that great English king. Henry's memorable St. Crispin's Day speech in this play has stirred students of Shakespeare for generations.

Only ninety years earlier than Leyte, on 25 October 1854, at Balaclava, the Light Brigade of English cavalry made its famous charge "into the valley of Death" against the vastly superior Russian army during the Crimean War. What reader has not been moved by the eloquent language of Alfred Lord Tennyson's poetic account of the gallantry displayed by the 600 British soldiers on that occasion?

The valor displayed by the Americans that morning off Samar is well depicted through the eyes of the men on the *Samuel B. Roberts*, who fought to the finish against overwhelming odds. In dealing with their heroism and devotion to duty, this book will typify the action of all those little American ships in response to such a mighty Japanese threat. It is a worthy tale of "Duty, Honor, and Country," to be forever proudly remembered by all Americans.

— J. Henry Doscher, Jr.

Acknowledgments

It has been my pleasure to have received the assistance and guidance of various persons, not the least of whom are many former members of ship's company on the USS *Samuel B. Roberts.*

I am greatly indebted to Dr. Dean C. Allard, who, until his recent retirement, was the director of the U.S. Naval Historical Center, Washington Navy Yard, Washington, D.C. In addition, I received much advice and cooperation from Ms. Kathy Lloyd and Mr. Bernard Cavalcante and members of their staff in the Operational Archives of the Historical Center.

As with my earlier book, I have again received significant assistance and advice from Mr. Richard A. von Doenhoff, Military Reference Branch, Textual Reference Division, National Archives I, Pennsylvania Avenue, Washington, D.C. Mr. Fred Pernell and members of the staff of National Archives II, at College Park, Maryland, were most helpful in furnishing many of the photographs used in this book.

Others who furnished data or made records available include: Ms. Helen B. McDonald, Admiral Nimitz Museum, Fredericksburg, Texas; Mr. H. S. (Gus) Edwards of Abilene, Texas, who died in January 1996; Mr. H. Whitney Felt of Salt Lake City, Utah, president of the *Samuel B. Roberts* Survivors Association; Mr. Jack Yusen of Bellevue, Washington, president of the Taffy 3 Association; Mr. Rick Weatherl of Weatherl & Associates, Architects, of Abilene, Texas; Mrs. Robert W. Copeland of Tacoma, Washington; Mrs. Peggy Carr Dodd of Checotah, Oklahoma; Mr. Robert LeClercq of Wimberley, Texas; Mr. J. Dudley Moylan of Minneapolis, Minnesota; Mr. Percell L. Worley of Hanover, Pennsylvania; Mr. Fred P. Nickless of Manchester, Massachusetts; Mr. Vincent N. Goodrich of Bradford, Pennsylvania; Ms. Lenora Rose Love of Dallas, Texas; and Mr. William Francis Cordner, former fellow student at Amherst College who served as aviation ordnance officer on the USS *Gambier Bay* that fateful 25 October 1944.

Also, I express sincere appreciation for the exceptional speakers at the Admiral Nimitz Symposium at Kerrville, Texas, in October 1994, concerning the war in the Pacific during 1944. Those lecturers, which included the eminent historian John Costello, various surviving participants of the Battle of Leyte Gulf, and two former Japanese naval officers of that era, so piqued my interest in what occurred off Samar that I was stirred to write this manuscript from the vantage point of the "Little Wolf" which gave its all. Months of research, followed by numerous drafts, ensued.

Special gratitude is due to those who have proofread and critiqued my manuscript, especially Ms. Ruth Hatcher Williamson and Ms. Gwen Choate Smith, both of Abilene, Texas.

To all of the above, I am forever grateful.

1

Prelude

By late 1943, the industrial arm of the United States began to spew out ships and equipment in unbelievable volumes. The needs of the navy for great numbers of ships to handle convoy duty had prompted the development of various type of new craft. Among these was a category designated "destroyer escorts," known generally as DEs.

A destroyer escort was, in a sense, a stripped-down version of a destroyer. Designed to be built rather quickly, the DE was thin-skinned, with limited armament, a smaller power plant, and minimum equipment. It displaced only 1,275 tons, about sixty-five percent as much as that of a true destroyer. For armanent it had two 5-inch/38 guns, one forward, one aft; two 40mm and six 20mm guns; depth charges; and three torpedo tubes. Thus it was as lightly armed as it was built. In very crowded quarters it carried a complement of eleven officers and 219 enlisted men. Many of the men did not even have bunks; rather, they slept in hammocks which were swung each time used. Everyone lived and worked in very cramped quarters on a destroyer escort.

In order to have such ships rapidly built in great numbers, the navy encouraged the development of new shipyards. One of these was the Brown Shipbuilding Company on the banks of the Houston Ship Channel near the Texas coast. These new entrepreneurs of shipbuilding, not constricted by the methods historically used for ship construction, were very innovative in the techniques they employed. Similar to the manufacturing methods developed by legendary Henry J. Kaiser, the Brown Shipbuilding Company made great use of prefabrication in an assembly line mode of operation. In slightly more than five months, Brown could fully complete a destroyer escort. That was a truly remarkable feat.

The Brown Shipyard laid the keels of two DEs on 6 December 1943, one of which was the *Samuel B. Roberts*, numbered 413. This class of ships honored the memory of enlisted men who had distinguished themselves in enemy action. The *Roberts* was named for Samuel Booker Roberts, Jr., of Portland, Oregon, a navy coxswain who had been awarded, posthumously, the Navy Cross for extraordinary heroism at Guadalcanal on 27 September 1942.

The *Roberts* was launched into the Houston Ship Channel on 20 January 1944, and Mrs. Samuel B. Roberts, then of Kansas City, Missouri, duly christened the vessel in honor of her son. Thereafter, the ship was fully completed and placed in commission on 28 April 1944.

On 4 March 1944, LCDR Robert W. Copeland, who was to be the commanding officer, arrived in Houston. He joined Lt. Lloyd A. Gurnett and Lt. (jg) William S. Burton, son of Senator Burton from Ohio, soon to be Associate Justice Burton of the United States Supreme Court. Gurnett and Burton had been at the shipyard about two weeks. Soon these three officers were joined by Lt. Trowbridge, the engineering officer, Lt. (jg) Tom Stevenson, the communications officer, and thirty enlisted men who were the nucleus of the crew. These initial officers and men were the personnel assigned for duty during the final construction phase and basic fitting-out of the *Roberts*.

The remainder of the enlisted precommissioning detail was assembled at Norfolk, Virginia, together with Ensigns John S. LeClercq and John Dudley Moylan. At Norfolk the navy conducted a special training school for crews assigned to the destroyer escorts. Some of these men had prior navy duty; others had recently completed various navy Class "A" schools pertaining to a particular rating, such as Sonar School or Radar School. A few were fresh out of boot camp. Fortunately, many had been through the Submarine Chaser Training Center at Miami, Florida. The specialized training at Norfolk was completed in early April, and the group of about 190 men were transferred to Houston on their own troop train. Ensign LeClercq was placed in charge of the train, and Ensign Moylan volunteered to go along to assist him.

As with most troop trains during the war, much time was spent on sidings, since freight and passenger trains had priority. The train left Norfolk in the afternoon and finally reached Rockymount, North Carolina, shortly after midnight. There had been no food along the way and the hungry crew was ready for a good meal. Sitting in the railyard was a greasy spoon cafe used by train crews, with only one cook on duty. The crew swamped this little place, but typical of what later would be called the "Sammy-B Spirit," the navy cooks in that crew, headed by Fred A. Strehle SC1c, turned to and took over the kitchen, overwhelming the lone, amazed, civilian cook. In short order the crew was fed a great meal, amid much hilarity. With the troop train signaling imminent departure, all hands left the restaurant and climbed aboard.

The train proceeded slowly into South Carolina, through Florence, and on to Orangeburg, the hometown of one member of the crew, Lin S. Ferris, Bkr2c. Somehow the conductor of the train had alerted Lin's family, and they, along with many of his friends, were lined up on the station platform when the troop train arrived. They gave him and the crew a grand reception, which one survivor has described to me as "most moving and memorable." After that brief but joyous meeting, the men climbed on board and the train was off to Atlanta, Georgia.

At the station in Atlanta, the men had to march downtown to one of the restaurants used by troop trains. It proved to be a real test for Ensign LeClercq; for, in spite of his vigorous protests, that restaurant would not allow the few blacks in the crew to be served. In the days of segregation, Atlanta made no exception for the military. Thus, John LeClercq had to have the black men in the crew march to another restaurant located elsewhere in town. As more than one survivor has reported, it was a tragic experience that continued to haunt John severely thereafter.

As the troop train continued its slow crawl through Alabama and Mississippi, it was often shunted onto sidings. On one such occasion, they had to wait several hours in a very isolated rural area where cows were grazing in a nearby pasture. Since more than one crew member had experienced bullriding, two or three men climbed on the cows and attempted to ride them, to the amusement of their buddies. There was much whooping and hollering by the onlookers, especially each time a rider was thrown off or fell from a cow. It was a moment of carefree fun which helped to relieve the monotony of a lengthy trip on a slow troop train.

At last, after five long and tiring days, the train arrived in Houston, where the weather was warm and inviting. It was a relief to be off of that old train, a relic from the turn of the century. Typical of many troop trains, it was made up of old equipment — chair cars, long ago abandoned but recalled to wartime duty after being only slightly refurbished. The men vividly recall the straight, hardback wooden seats, the potbellied stoves for heating, and the ancient gas lanterns used for interior lighting. It was a chore to get any sleep during that long, tiresome trip. Furthermore, all baggage was locked in a special car, so the only clothes they had for the trip were those that they were wearing when the train left Norfolk. As one man reported, although they were indeed a smelly bunch when the train arrived in Houston, they all were in good spirits. Detraining, the officers were sent to the Rice Hotel for billeting, while the crew boarded special buses for a short ride to the precommissioning barracks located at the Brown Shipyard.

Shortly they would see the ship that would be their home — and, as fate would have it, ultimately the grave for many of them — in a most heroic battle soon to occur off Samar at Leyte Gulf.

2

Houston

After the crew which had been assembled in Norfolk arrived in Houston in mid-April, only about two weeks remained until the finishing touches in the construction of the *Roberts* were completed and the ship was ready to be commissioned into the navy. During this final stage of work, the ship was at the fitting out piers where special equipment of all types was being installed. It was a busy time as the shipyard personnel worked feverishly to meet the 28 April target date.

During this interim, the crew was getting acquainted with the ship. Because of their special training at Norfolk, which included exposure to DEs, most of the crew already knew the layout of their new duty stations. They and the officers constantly checked everything, making certain that equipment was properly constructed and installed. There were the usual arguments with the builders and the inspectors, particularly since these ships were "slapped together" in great haste. Three shifts, around the clock, were standard for the shipyard workers. Officers and crew had to check out everything that was installed, for if something was not done correctly in the shipyard, it would be difficult to have it straightened out later. Thus, the crew stayed busy as the civilian workers, and there was not much time for liberty.

A few days prior to 28 April, the living quarters were completed to such an extent that some of the crew were moved aboard. Vast quantities of stores and all types of supplies had to be obtained from the shipyard warehouses and placed on board the ship. There was a light rail line from the warehouse area to the dock alongside the ship, and on it was a railroad flatcar. The crew would load the supplies onto the flatcar and then push it the short distance to the pier where the ship was docked. It was a back-breaking job, but, with the "gung-ho" spirit of this crew, all was accomplished in due time. Once the stores were aboard, the remainder of the crew left the barracks and moved into their quarters on the *Roberts*.

A few days before the commissioning ceremony, the remaining officers arrived at the shipyard. These included the newly designated executive officer, Lt. E. E. Roberts, Jr.; Lt. C. M. Ulrich, gunnery officer; and Ens. L. P. Riebenbauer, assistant engineering officer. Ensign LeClercq became the assistant gunnery officer and Ensign Moylan was designated the radar and sound officer. The ship now had its full complement of officers and crew.

Dockside, on 28 April 1944, a beautiful spring day, at 1630 prompt, the formal ceremony occurred whereby the ship was commissioned into service as part of the fleet. Officers and crew, resplendent in their dress white uniforms, stood at attention as Capt. DeWitt C. Redgrave USN came aboard. He represented the commandant, Eighth Naval District, and duly read the orders whereby the navy accepted and commissioned the ship as the USS *Samuel B. Roberts*. In turn, LCDR Robert Copeland read his orders detailing him as commanding officer. With the national ensign hoisted aft, the Union Jack at the bow, and the commission pennant raised to the truck of the mast, the initial watch section was posted to duty.

Mrs. Samuel B. Roberts, mother of Samuel B. Roberts, Jr., had planned to attend this ceremony, but heavy rains in the Midwest had sent the rivers in the Kansas City area on such a rampage she was prevented from getting to Houston.

However, family and friends of some of the officers and crew attended this ceremony. It was a proud moment for all of them. Among such guests were the parents of Ensign LeClercq, who came down from Dallas, and the parents of Lieutenant (jg) Stevenson from Manhasset, Long Island, New York. The Stevenson family has long been in the shipping business; their freighters haul cargo around the world even to this day. Thus Mr. Stevenson took special delight in checking out the entire ship and was greatly impressed with the cleanliness of the engine rooms and the efficient use of the limited space everywhere.

For the next few days, all equipment was checked for proper functioning, and dock trials of the main engines were conducted.

With everything in order, it was time to depart the shipyard and proceed to Galveston for extensive sea trials. Accordingly, on 3 May, at 1259, with everyone again in dress white uniforms and the crew manning the rail, the *Roberts* pulled smartly away from the pier and into the narrow Houston Ship Channel. As the officer of the deck on that occasion reported, the skipper's prior DE experience involved ships with diesel engines. Diesel-powered ships respond immediately to changes in direction and speed. The *Roberts* was a straight steam job, Westinghouse geared turbine, and such a ship responds slowly to ordered changes in direction. A bit of humor resulted. Such officer stated:

> We were pulling away from the fitting out dock, everyone smartly dressed in white uniforms, as all of the shipyard workers assembled on the dock watched and cheered us on. The Captain had previously had command of a diesel powered DE, but had no experience with steam turbine powered vessels. At that time, I was the officer of the deck during special sea detail, and the skipper ordered both engines full astern. As you know, the Houston Ship Channel is not very wide, and we started approaching the opposite shore at a pretty good rate of speed. The Captain did not realize that it takes some time to reverse a steam turbine as compared to a diesel engine, and although he got the screws turning forward at full speed ahead, we were already up in the marshy meadow. Now cows that were grazing there were running for their lives. Then the ship, finally responding to the engine order of full speed ahead, picked up speed and headed for the dock where about two thousand shipyard workers now began running for their lives. We finally got the ship safely underway, and proceeded down the ship channel to the San Jacinto Ordnance Depot to take on our allotment of ammunition, en route to Galveston.

With this almost tragic, but humorous, episode behind them, Galveston and very detailed sea trials and gunnery tests next awaited the men of the "Sammy-B."

3

Galveston and Bermuda

Even though it is only about a fifty-mile trip from the Port of Houston to Galveston, the ship did not arrive in Galveston until late the afternoon of 5 May. Upon reaching the San Jacinto Ordnance Deport, en route to Galveston, a water leak developed in the magazine sprinkling system in compartment A-204L. Pipefitters were called from the Brown Shipyard to repair the defect. This took all the next day. Therefore, ammunition could not be safely loaded on board until the morning of 5 May. With this completed, the ship departed the ordnance depot and continued on its trip to Galveston, where it moored port side to Pier Charlie of Todd Shipyard. Two days were involved in additional fitting out of the ship. When that work was finished, the ship moved to Pier 41 in the city of Galveston at 1638, and two sections of the crew were granted liberty until midnight.

On 10 May the ship stood out of Galveston Harbor to compensate the compass. Returning to Pier 37 at 1840, part of the crew again had a short liberty. During the next two days, the ship went out into the Gulf of Mexico and conducted structural firing tests of all guns as well as engine and ship control tests. These were detailed tests, with naval and civilian inspectors aboard. The engines were tested severely — full speed ahead, then full speed astern, then full speed ahead, several times. The rudder was moved sharply to port, then to starboard, then to port, repeatedly. As a result, the ship and its equipment were put through grueling tests to ensure that certain critical machinery and equipment would not fail, even under the most trying circumstances. During these trials a crack was found in the casing of the #2 boiler in a fireroom. To correct this, they returned to port the afternoon of 12 May, and the ship tied up at Todd Shipyard's Pier "D." Workmen immediately began around-the-clock efforts to replace the cracked casing.

These repairs finally accomplished, the ship moved to the fuel docks at noon on 15 May. With fueling completed at 1423, the captain reported to the navy that the ship was ready for sea in all respects. At last, the *Roberts* was under way for Bermuda, clearing the Galveston Harbor entrance buoy shortly after 1820, and was out to sea before sunset.

As scheduled, they rendezvoused with the USS *Cronin* (DE-704) the next day, and together the two ships then proceeded to Bermuda. Each day and each night during the six-day trip, these two ships conducted various tactical exercises. This gave the younger officers a chance to gain practical experience in shiphandling maneuvers, and enabled all hands to become familiar with their ship and its capabilities. Each day the crew exercised and participated in drills at general quarters; everyone was becoming acquainted with his job, his station, and his function at each drill. It was a time for confidence building, and was excellent preparation for the drills which they would encounter during the shakedown procedures awaiting them in Bermuda.

On 17 May at 2005 they sighted Loggerhead Key buoy, left the Gulf of Mexico through the Florida Straits, rounded the Florida Keys, and then proceeded a short distance up the lower eastern coastal areas of Florida. With the benefit of the Gulf Stream their speed increased slightly, and in the early morning on 21 May Bermuda was sighted. The *Roberts* entered the harbor, and by 1039 moored alongside the USS *Hamul*, a destroyer tender, in Great Sound. Later that day they loaded hedgehog ammunition and took on fuel. Officers and crew had one day to relax before their shakedown trials were to commence.

For nearly a month, the ship put to sea on most days and on a few nights to participate in every type of drill imaginable. These included torpedo exercises, hedgehog and depth charge attacks on some Italian submarines the United States had acquired, target practice with all guns, and tactical drills with other ships. They even conducted fueling-at-sea maneuvers and abandon-ship procedures. Many DEs were involved in these exercises.

In the various gunnery drills, a large target is towed behind a tugboat, a procedure especially useful for night firing practice. One crewman recalls an evening when the lead ship in the formation initially mistook the tug for the target, but just in time the tug made itself known before any shots were fired. As he related:

> We were having night firing practice; our whole group of DEs was to open fire on the target which was on a barge being towed by the tug. The first ship was to illuminate the target with star shells, and the rest of us were then to open fire. All of a sudden the "target" lit up and all sorts of lights were flashing, etc. The star shells had illuminated the tug, not the target!

No doubt the crews on the tugs involved in this type of duty kept a wary eye on the somewhat green crews going through shakedown drills. In this instance they certainly did, and promptly set off all the warning bells, whistles, and blinking lights.

Most evenings, and on every Sunday, the ships were in port and the officers and crews had some liberty ashore. The citizens of Bermuda were friendly and helpful, which made the time there pleasant and memorable. Transportation on this island was generally by bicycle or train. One petty officer related:

> I recall renting bicycles, putting them on a train and riding to the end of the line with fellow crewmen. We found a small restaurant out there and I sampled my first ginger beer. The beauty of that island, with the pastel colored homes, has always stayed with me. I'm sorry I was never able to return there.

A young ensign reported that he thoroughly enjoyed his first gin and tonic at the bar of the Yacht Club, since such a drink had not yet become popular in the USA.

While all was not work during that month at Bermuda, nevertheless, with hard work and devotion to duty, the men of the "Sammy-B" quickly became a seasoned team. This rigorous shakedown training would serve them well in the months to come. On 19

June, upon conclusion of the exercises, Capt. D. L. Madiera USN, commander of the DD-DE Shakedown Training Group, Bermuda, came aboard for the final inspection of the ship and its men. He was highly complimentary, and they were given an outstanding grade on their performance.

After Captain Madiera left the ship, the *Roberts* got under way at 1540 for Boston. As they sailed past the ship of the commodore for their DE squadron, the commodore had a Tare, Victor, George flag hoist raised. Every navy man knows this translates in the Signal Book to "Well Done."

With pride, they were on their way.

4

Boston, Norfolk, and Pearl Harbor

During a portion of the trip to Boston, the *Roberts* escorted an ancient Hudson River dayliner, the *Berkshire*. It was being towed to Norfolk by an ocean-going tugboat and could only make three or four knots an hour. Going was very slow and the sea was rough. At one point the *Berkshire* reported that it was taking on water and might sink. Permission was requested of Washington to abandon the old dayliner. This request was denied, since the old vessel had great quantities of brass railings, then a critical item for ammunition. It was to be taken to Norfolk to salvage this material. Fortunately, the men on the *Berkshire* ultimately managed to stop the leaks and pump out enough water to stay afloat. On 24 June the tug and its tow were dropped off at Cape Henry, Virginia, near Norfolk, and the *Roberts* then proceeded alone to Boston.

On 26 June, at 0833, the ship entered Boston Harbor and tied up to Pier 6, South Boston Navy Yard, where it had ten days of postshakedown availability. Much work had to be done correcting some flaws which became apparent after departing Galveston. In addition, the ship was completely repainted with a camouflage design, as it was now destined to join the Pacific Fleet.

The shipyard had three shifts, working night and day, and civilian workers were all over the ship. One member of the crew discovered that workmen, doing some welding near his locker, burned all of his uniforms which were inside. From a supply officer he obtained a detailed breakdown of the cost of the uniforms and made a complaint to the foreman. Even though there was no insurance coverage, the foreman took up a collection from the civilian workers and fully reimbursed the grateful young sailor.

The character of the work made the ship quite dirty, and the constant noise of work around-the-clock made it difficult to sleep. All the inconvenience was worth it for, upon completion, they had a much improved ship. Among these improvements were more bunks to accommodate some of the men who had been sleeping in hammocks.

During the shipyard availability, the crew was divided into two sections, with each section getting four days' leave. Those men not on leave, and not on night duty, received liberty in Boston each evening. The short stay there afforded the crew their last real liberty and leave for months to come. Since there was almost no airline service available, most of the crew could not visit at home unless they lived nearby. Some took the train to New York City, as many had never been there; others spent their leave in Boston, a great place for liberty during the war. The men of the "Sammy-B" enjoyed this historic city to the fullest. The ten days at South Boston Navy Yard passed all too quickly.

While in Boston, a few members of the crew were transferred, and some new members came on board. In fact, the skipper managed to obtain more men than were allotted to a DE, making conditions aboard even more crowded. One additional officer who came aboard was a physician, Lt. (jg) D. M. Ervin (MC) USNR. On 28 June he reported for duty, and remained with the ship until it joined its squadron in the far Pacific.

On 7 July, at 0732, the *Roberts* got under way to calibrate the compass as it cleared the harbor. Upon successful completion of the calibration, the ship's orders directed it to proceed to Pearl Harbor via the Panama Canal and to pick up some other ships at Norfolk while en route. But as fate would have it, as we shall see, a long stop at Norfolk would become necessary.

Once the navy team who calibrated the compass just outside the entrance to Boston Harbor departed the ship by motor launch, the *Roberts* was under way alone. It was a beautiful clear day and the men not on watch were enjoying some relaxation as the ship sailed through calm seas. Suddenly, off Cape Cod, while Ensign LeClercq was officer of the deck, the sonar operator on duty called out "good contact, 400 yards, up doppler." An object was approaching the ship. Hearing this shout, LCDR Copeland, the skipper, who was nearby, raced to ring up "back full" on the engine order telegraph which was located on the bridge. Before this could be done, there was a resounding crash, followed by an even more violent crash. There was no need to sound the general alarm since every man who was not on watch immediately raced topside to his General Quarters (GQ) station.

As it turned out, the ship had been attacked or hit from just below the surface of the ocean by a whale measuring at least sixty feet long! As the whale slid down the starboard side of the ship, it came in contact with the starboard screw. This was the cause of the second crash. The sharp blades of the screw cut through the backbone of the whale, and as it surfaced, a geyser of blood rose some five feet from his back; an amazing sight.

Needless to say, many of the crew not on duty first thought the ship had been torpedoed by a German U-boat. As one young seaman reported:

> The big scare that we had was on our trip south from Boston.
> While some of us were relaxing and finally enjoying some leisure
> time, there was what sounded like a big explosion. The ship just
> shook and rattled. Everyone took off for topside, thinking that we
> had been hit by a torpedo. After reaching topside and our G.Q.
> stations, we were informed we had been rammed by a whale. This
> gave us something to talk about the rest of the trip.

The ship then limped into Norfolk for repairs, arriving late on 9 July. It was necessary to have the starboard screw replaced, as well as a portion of the sound dome of the sonar gear located underwater. While in drydock, some pieces of whale flesh were recovered from the area of the damaged starboard screw. The work done in the drydock was completed in a few days, and the ship moved to Pier 23, Naval Operating Base, Norfolk.

The last evening the ship was in Norfolk it obtained a mascot. The skipper and the first lieutenant were returning to the ship after midnight when they spotted a small black dog on the pier. Apparently it had been abandoned and was looking for anyone who might befriend it. On the spur of the moment they decided to take the dog aboard, and carried it to the wardroom. They aroused Lt. (jg) Ervin, the ship's doctor, and had him check over the dog. Approved as fit for duty, the dog became part of ship's company. He was given the name "Sammy," and, out of jest, a service record was created for him. Sammy soon became well acquainted with each area of the ship and with the men of the "Sammy-B."

Finally, on 22 July, with everything in readiness, the *Roberts* departed Norfolk for the Canal Zone in company with the USS *Monitor* (LSV-5), the USS *Chara* (AKA-58), and the USS *Nawmann* (DE-416). These ships constituted Task Unit 29.6.2. Because of the continuing U-boat menace, the ships zigzagged the entire trip.

The ships arrived safely at Cristobal, Canal Zone, in the early morning, 27 July, and at once began their trip through the canal. The transit took almost six hours, and at 1538 they entered the Miraflores Locks by which they were lowered into the salt water of Balboa Harbor on the Pacific side of Panama. Soon they tied up to Pier 1, Balboa.

While everyone was awestruck by the Panama Canal, many in the crew vividly remember the heat and humidity. Navy ships were not then air conditioned; spaces below deck were cramped; fresh air blower systems were not designed for the tropics. Thus, when in tropical areas, many men slept and stayed topside where it was cooler.

The ship was only at Balboa overnight, but half of the crew was granted liberty until midnight. Some bought souvenirs; all drank beer, some drank lots of beer. Some were heckled by "three-dollar" prostitutes who shouted the vilest obscenities from their doors or windows. One seventeen-year-old seaman, who was not in the liberty section, was on duty at the quarterdeck when liberty expired. He reported:

> I didn't have liberty that night, but those that did had a ball. I was on the quarterdeck watch when the men in the liberty section started returning to the ship. Some came back with no help, some with help, and a few with shore patrol escort. Some of the stories they told were pretty amazing. At Balboa we found out what some people would do for the "Yankee Dolla."

For those who managed to get ashore, Balboa amply provided

an opportunity for a final blast before departing for the unknown duties ahead. While many partook in such a wild night, no one has yet expressed a desire to return to Balboa.

Pursuant to ComPaSeaFron dispatch 281332, the *Roberts* was under way at 1612 on 28 July for Pearl Harbor with three other ships — the *Nawmann*, the *Monitor*, and the *Chara*. These four ships were designated as Task Unit 12.9.1. It was an uneventful trip, with good weather and calm seas. Each day the crew was exercised in various drills; otherwise it was a monotonous voyage.

During this segment of the trip, to help break the boredom, a ship's newspaper, the *GIZMO*, was created. Its first editor was the doctor who assembled a staff from all divisions of the ship. News articles, jokes, mini-biographies of personnel, even poems by shipmates were published. An issue came out each week, printed on a mimeograph machine, with the initial issue on 4 August. Through this publication, the crew learned more about their shipmates: where they came from, their families, their prior work and education.

For instance, they learned that the oldest man on the ship, Tullio J. Serafini RM1c, at forty-five years of age, had enlisted just in time to join the *Roberts*. He was born in Frontone, Italy, and had immigrated to the United States with his parents at the age of three. During World War I, being too young, he lied about his age in order to join the navy, having finally reached seventeen only when that war ended. In 1944, in order to serve in World War II, he again lied about his age — this time claiming to be younger than he was! There were others who were foreign born, such as Maurice Brodsky, S2c. As a youngster he had come to San Francisco with his parents from Kremachuk, Russia, to escape the revolution, via Leipzig, London, Paris, and Madrid. This crew typified the diversity of the American population and its armed forces.

Finally, on 10 August, after a long trip, the *Roberts* arrived at Pearl Harbor, and at 1645 it tied up alongside the USS *Fieberling* (DE-640) at the DE docks.

Soon the hazardous duty of the officers and crew of the *Roberts* would begin; duty for which they had so diligently trained, and for which they were now well prepared.

5

Eniwetok, Kwajalein, and Manus

During the remainder of August, all of September, and part of October, the *Roberts* escorted various troop and supply ships from Pearl Harbor to Eniwetok and Kwajalein in the Marshall Islands. This was done in preparation for the upcoming invasion of the Philippine Islands. Each round trip took about fifteen days, as supply ships were notoriously slow. On one of the return trips to Pearl, two new officers came aboard for duty: Ens. Jack K. Moore and Ens. Luther A. West.

Shortly after midnight on one trip, while traveling without a convoy, Whit Felt SoM3c, who was standing watch at the sonar gear on the bridge, had an excellent, sharp echo. He notified Lieutenant Gurnett, then the officer of the deck, who immediately turned on the antisubmarine recorder. Its tracings indicated a solid contact, possibly that of a submarine. Promptly Lieutenant Gurnett headed toward the target, was upon it in seconds, and immediately ordered the dropping of depth charges and the firing of K-guns. Only then did he sound the general alarm; however, it was hardly necessary as the men, awakened by the first explosion, bumped into each other in the darkened ship while rushing to their GQ stations. The skipper, in his skivvies, rushed to the bridge to ask for an explanation. Lieutenant Gurnett informed him that there was no time to apprise him of the situation, that they were on the target instantly. The skipper accepted this explanation for he realized that Lieutenant Gurnett and Felt had taken the correct action. A search was continued, but no target was picked up again on the sonar equipment. What produced that fine echo is not known to this day.

Upon each return to Pearl, the *Roberts* had a couple of days in port. Each section of the crew received a brief time ashore during the day from 0900 to 1600 hours. In the morning, the liberty sections were carried by boats from the ship to landings near Pearl City. The men then had to wait in line for buses to take them to Honolulu. This procedure was reversed on the return trip. Lines, and more lines, were everywhere for everything. One crewman reported that men stood in line for beer, for buses, and for boats. There even were lines for those who went to various bordellos. Thus, time to relax ashore was rather brief and certainly frustrating.

Other members of the crew went to Waikiki Beach and visited the beach hotels or just walked around Honolulu. One young crewman reported:

> It was exciting to visit Waikiki Beach and see all of those fancy hotels and places I had heard about, but after two or three trips ashore even that became boring. Ray Youngblood and I decided to ride a city bus into the hills behind the city for a view of the ocean. We got off of the bus at the end of the line and walked through a beautiful residential area. I remember talking to several Hawaiians who were working in their gardens or washing their cars. They were surprised to see two sailors in dress whites so far from the heart of Honolulu. One man and his wife asked us into their home and we ate with them. They all were appreciative of the job they felt we were doing to protect their island from falling into enemy hands.

While Honolulu did not offer much for the brief time the men had liberty, there was absolutely nothing at Eniwetok or Kwajalein except beer halls. At Eniwetok on 31 August, the crew organized two softball teams and went ashore at 1430 for some recreation and exercise. The 7 September issue of the *GIZMO*, now edited by Ensign Moylan (Lt. (jg) Ervin, the doctor, had been transferred to the division flagship), related on its sports page:

Twenty-two men (and one umpire) braved the scorching sun to engage in a bang-up softball game Thursday, 31 August. It was a clash of Goldie Goldstein's Goons against Red Harrington's All Stars. The game was sparked by sensational hitting, fielding, and base running to assure an 11-4 victory for the Goons.

A crowd of approximately 5000 sailors and marines witnessed the spectacle (from a distance) and the calm air was filled with rousing cheers and shouts of joy (and the odor of beer).

The highlights of the game included "Fatty" Walsh's terrific home run, Goldstein's double, "Brancato" Paone playing bang-up defensive ball throughout, and Ooten's sensational "steal" from 1st to 3rd, directly. He maintained, to no avail, the shortest distance between two points is a straight line!

The game's only casualty came when "Husky Harvey" Hinken and "Two Knife" Tony Schaffer collided in an attempt to catch a long fly between center and left field. "Two Knife" caught the ball.

As events developed, this was the last carefree moment of relaxation for the men of the DE-413.

Soon they began escorting a convoy to Manus in the Admiralty Islands, located about two degrees south of the equator. Members of a ship's company who have never crossed the equator are known as "Pollywogs." Those who have been across are called "Shellbacks." Ceremonies have traditionally existed in the navy to initiate "Pollywogs" into the Ancient Order of the Deep. Due homage is paid to King Neptune at the behest of Davy Jones.

Only three officers and about thirty members of the crew were "Shellbacks," and they conducted the initiation. The evening before the ceremonies, King Neptune decreed that the "Shellbacks" would have steak with all the trimmings for dinner, but the "Pollywogs" would have only beans, bread, and water. The next morning, as the ship crossed the Equator, the hazing of the "Pollywogs" began in earnest. Many have told me that it was quite an initiation, one they have never forgotten. A few old scores were settled between some of the men.

Upon reaching Manus the next morning, the *Roberts* joined a mighty armada. The ships and the troops for the invasion of the Philippines were gathered here and at Hollandia, New Guinea. Seeadler Harbor at Manus is enormous, as large as any in the Pacific Ocean. The crew were awestruck by the magnitude of the ships riding at anchor in this serene harbor. They sailed past hundreds of ships, as they made their way to the assigned anchorage. There were numerous "Jeep" aircraft carriers, many battleships, cruisers, destroyers, destroyer escorts, landing craft of all types, patrol craft, subchasers, rocket launchers, tankers, supply ships, and troop transports. After topping off their fuel tanks at an oiler, they tied up alongside the DE-412, a sister ship from the Brown Shipyard.

For several days, LCDR Copeland, the skipper, attended a series of conferences and briefings relating to the upcoming invasion. He was given three copies of the top-secret operation order for "King Musketeer II," code name for this invasion. One copy he gave to Lt. E. E. Roberts, the executive officer; another went to Lt. (jg) Tom Stevenson, the communications officer, so he could set up the communication plan. The third copy he kept to study personally. An operation order for a major engagement, such as this one for the invasion of the Philippines, is very detailed and must be studied with great care to be completely understood.

Time was now short. In just a matter of a few days, these hundreds of ships would be under way for Leyte, the initial place chosen for the long-awaited return of the American forces to the Philippines.

Everyone on the "Sammy-B" waited anxiously, for they knew the next move would be their supreme test. They were ready.

6

Manus to Leyte

The more than 700 ships gathered at Manus to participate in the invasion of Leyte were now part of the Seventh Fleet, under the command of Vice Adm. Thomas C. Kincaid. This fleet constituted the navy of Gen. Douglas MacArthur, commander in chief Southwest Pacific Area, and thus its top commander. The ships were on loan from the Third Fleet, under the command of Adm. William F. Halsey. The Third Fleet was under the overall command of Adm. Chester W. Nimitz, commander in chief Pacific Fleet and Pacific Ocean Areas.

This division of top commands was to become a critical "flaw" in the succeeding turn of events at Leyte, as President Roosevelt had declined to place a coordinating superior over these two commanders who were considered supreme in their respective areas of operations. The Philippine Islands were in MacArthur's area. He was assigned the Seventh Fleet, which would carry out the naval aspects of the invasion; Halsey and his Third Fleet, under Nimitz, would "lend support" to the operations.

Within this newly "beefed up" Seventh Fleet at Manus were eighteen escort carriers (CVEs), known among naval personnel as

"Jeep carriers" or "baby flattops." Assigned to them were nine destroyers (DDs) and sixteen destroyer escorts (DEs), to serve as an antisubmarine screen and a pilot rescue force. This entire group of ships was designated Task Group 77.4 under the command of Rear Adm. T. L. Sprague. The *Roberts* became part of this Task Group.

Other Task Groups in the Seventh Fleet consisted of restored battleships, along with cruisers, transports, destroyers, supply ships, minesweepers, and various other types of ships. Some of these were gathered at Hollandia, in New Guinea, mainly amphibious landing craft and supporting transports.

Together, all of the ships in the Seventh Fleet constituted three Task Forces — 77, 78, and 79.

About 800 miles to the north of Manus and 900 miles east of Leyte lies Ulithi Atoll, with a magnificent large, deep harbor. This is where Admiral Halsey's Third Fleet, comprising Task Force 38, sortied. It consisted of the largest, most modern, and fastest ships of their class in the navy. Numbering some sixteen carriers, a half-dozen battleships, fifteen cruisers, and more than forty-five destroyers, it was a formidable aggregation of naval power. Added to the ships of the Seventh Fleet, the combined forces were greater than had been assembled at Normandy. The Third Fleet was directed by Nimitz to support the invasion of the Philippines and to destroy Japanese naval and air forces in that area. A debated addition to this order provided that if an opportunity for the destruction of a major portion of the enemy fleet occurred, that destruction would become a primary task. This opened the door for the events which led to the action off Samar and the loss of the *Roberts*, other ships, and many lives. Without it, the events that nurtured this book could not have occurred.

The date for the actual landing of troops in the invasion of Leyte was set for 20 October 1944, designated in the operation order as A-Day. All days in that order were referred to as A minus 1 or 2 or 3, or A plus 1, etc. The *Roberts* and the rest of its Task Group 77.4 were directed to be in the Leyte Gulf area at A minus 3, or 17 October. Along with some 700 ships, comprising many Task Groups and Task Units, the *Roberts* set sail from Manus the morning of 12 October, destination Leyte Gulf. Two days earlier the force of minesweepers had departed, in order to sweep Leyte Gulf and the nearby areas of enemy mines. Simultaneously, the ships at Hollandia departed, fully loaded with troops and equipment. Admiral Halsey's Third Fleet Task Force 38 was already at sea, and had made devastating air attacks on Formosa. Now, on 17 October, Halsey's ships began their maneuvers to support the Leyte landings which were to occur three days hence. Thus, all of the naval forces which had gathered at Ulithi, Manus, and Hollandia were now converging on the Leyte area of the Philippines.

During the trip from Manus to Leyte, the *Roberts* and its group encountered a typhoon which slowed their movement. The account of LCDR Copeland, commanding officer of the *Roberts*, was included in an unpublished manuscript:

> I have been in many storms . . . but this was no storm . . . this was a genuine typhoon. We got wind gusts up to ninety miles an hour. . . . We plowed right into the middle of the storm. . . .
>
> It got to the point where it was actually hazardous to try and relieve the watches or to be out on deck trying to move. . . . A lot of the crew were down in their bunks, sick, almost ready to die. . . . The seas were so rough and the ship pounded so badly that for the first two or three hours many of the crew were afraid the ship would sink. For the next sixteen or eighteen hours many of them were so sick that they were afraid she wouldn't sink. We took two rolls of fifty-five degrees, according to the inclinometer, which means it was easier at the end of a roll to stand on the bulkhead than it was to stand on the deck.

Several of the survivors have confirmed the ferocity of this storm and the difficulty of maneuvering the ship and remaining on station in the formation of ships. Ensign Moylan related:

> When we ran into that typhoon, the Officer of the Deck, which sometimes was me, was the only person actually outside. And it was nervous watching the device that measured the roll of the ship to the side. The only thing I can remember eating was a handful of bread just pulled from a loaf.

Delayed by this typhoon for one day, they arrived at the Leyte Gulf area on 18 October, A-Day minus 2. Their Task Group 77.4 was divided into three Task Units, which, locally, became known by their voice radio call signs as Taffy 1, Taffy 2, and Taffy 3. The *Roberts* became part of Taffy 3, officially designated as Task Unit 77.4.3, under the immediate command of Rear Adm. C.A.F. Sprague. Taffy 3 was composed of six Jeep carriers — the *Fanshaw Bay*, *St. Lo*, *White Plains*, *Kalinin Bay*, *Kitkun Bay*, and *Gambier Bay*; three destroyers — *Hoel, Herrmann,* and *Johnston*; and four destroyer escorts — *Dennis, J.C. Butler, Raymond,* and *Samuel B. Roberts.* Taffy 3 was located just off the island of Samar, slightly to the northeast of Leyte Island and the entrance to Leyte Gulf. Taffy 2 was about twenty miles to the south, and Taffy 1 about forty miles to the south. Thus these three units were deployed in an area from just north of Leyte Gulf to just south of Leyte Gulf. Under this arrangement, the planes from the various Jeep carriers were in a good position to provide air reconnaissance and support for the landings which were to occur at Leyte Island on A-Day.

With these units in place, the bombardment and fire support ships arrived and began their extensive shelling of Japanese positions. This was a standard "softening-up" activity prior to any landing.

General MacArthur's celebrated "I shall return" to the Philippines was now imminent.

7

Leyte: Part I

At dawn on 20 October 1944, the fire support ships from the Seventh Fleet arrived at the entrance to Leyte Gulf. Entering the Gulf in force, great battleships — some restored veterans of the Pearl Harbor attack — opened the fierce shore bombardment that preceeded the troop landings. Admiral Halsey and his mighty Task Force 38 of the Third Fleet were standing by off nearby Samar to aid and assist the operations.

The bombardment by the Seventh Fleet continued until midmorning, and by 1000, as scheduled, the first assault waves went ashore in their myriad landing craft. The shore bombardments had accomplished their intended purpose; Japanese troops had fallen back, and our soldiers quickly established significant beachheads.

General MacArthur, embarked on his flagship USS *Nashville*, witnessed the landings. Shortly after lunch, he accomplished his famous return, wading ashore from a naval landing craft with some of his staff and President Osmena of the Philippines at his side. After a brief sojourn ashore, his prophetic declaration, "I shall return," accomplished, the general and his entourage returned to the cruiser

Nashville. The liberation of the Philippines was going according to schedule.

Because of Ranger reconnaissances at and near Leyte Gulf a few days prior to A-Day, the Japanese knew the area in which our operations would occur. With our landings at Leyte, the Japanese now placed into effect their war plan with the official code name of *Sho-Go*, which means "victory operation." It encompassed an "all or nothing" endeavor.

The Japanese Combined Command in Tokyo planned a daring feat for its navy — a plan that had a chance of success only if they could lure Admiral Halsey, with his huge carriers and fast ships, away from Leyte Gulf. Knowing his aggressive nature (he even had the nickname "Bull"), the Japanese felt their plan just might work.

This plan envisioned effecting a naval pincers movement on the American beachheads at Leyte, destroying the vast number of supply ships in Leyte Gulf, and bombarding our troops from the sea as Japanese land forces attacked from inland. A defeat of Americans at Leyte, combined with a massive destruction of our huge supplies and equipment assembled over a year for this huge operation, could overshadow Pearl Harbor. Any new invasion of the Philippines might be delayed a year, and the war with Japan could drag on. For this to occur less than two weeks prior to Roosevelt's hotly contested bid for a fourth term, the outcome of that presidential election just might be affected and a peace without unconditional surrender was possible. Thus bold action was the order of the day.

To accomplish such a pincers movement, one group of Japanese ships, the Center Force, would approach the area from the west, sail through the Sibuyan Sea, transit San Bernardino Strait, circle around Samar Island, and enter Leyte Gulf from the north. At the same time another naval force, the South Force, would approach from the west, sail through the Sulu Sea, into the Mindanao Sea, transit Surigao Strait, and enter Leyte Gulf from the south. In each instance a night passage of those two straits was planned to give some protection from American aircraft. As a result, the two naval forces would converge on Leyte Gulf at dawn to inflict a hoped-for massive carnage. However, as we shall see, concept and execution do not always mesh.

The Japanese had so few aircraft at this stage of the war, and so few aircraft carriers, there was no chance of even a suicide mission succeeding unless Halsey's mighty carriers and fast, modern cruis-

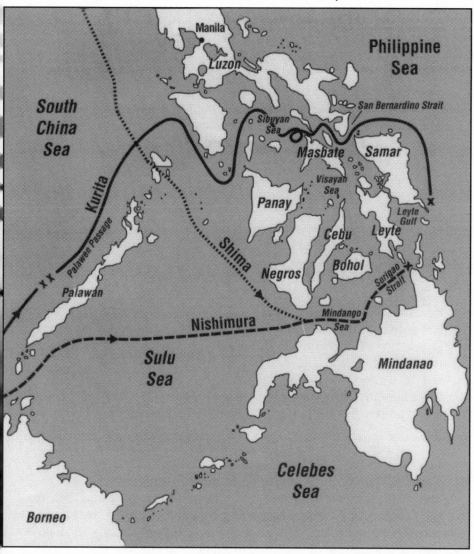

Track map of Japanese Center Force (Kurita) and Southern Force (Nishimura and Shima) in their Sho-go plan to crush our landing forces at Leyte. Kurita's track shows: ① the two "X" marks in Palawan Passage where our submarines *Darter* and *Dace* encountered Kurita on 23 October and sank three cruisers; ② the "loop" in Sibuyan Sea indicates area where Halsey's planes attacked Kurita on 24 October, causing Kurita to momentarily turn back. Once Halsey's planes departed, Kurita turned east again, passed through San Bernardino Strait that night and met Taffy 3 at dawn on 25 October. The "X" mark is the area of battle off Samar. The track map for Nishimura and Shima show their passage, and the "X" mark shows where they were soundly defeated by our Seventh Fleet in the Battle of Surigao Strait during the early morning hours of 25 October 1944. Based on three sighting maps prepared by H. S. (Gus) Edwards, former cartographic officer, for Seventh Fleet Intelligence.

ers, battleships, and destroyers were away from the Leyte area that dawn. Therefore, the Japanese created a third group of ships as "Halsey bait." The group comprised several aircraft carriers, with some supporting ships, which would approach the Philippine Sea from the north, considerably north of Luzon.

Above all, Halsey wanted to destroy the remaining Japanese aircraft carriers, so the Japanese Combined Command felt that he could be lured away from the Leyte Gulf area if he learned of such an enemy force. The "Bull" might just charge ahead!

The most potent Japanese naval group, referred to as the Center Force, was under the command of Vice Admiral Kurita. It was composed of seven battleships, thirteen cruisers, and some nineteen destroyers. After refueling at Brunei, the Center Force was directed to make the transit of San Bernardino Strait and enter the Philippine Sea around the north end of Samar.

The Japanese South Force was composed of two groups of ships. The main one was under the command of Vice Admiral Nishimura, which embarked for the Sulu Sea after refueling at Brunei. It had only two battleships, a cruiser, and four destroyers. It was to be joined in the Mindanao Sea by Vice Admiral Shima and his force of two battleships, a cruiser, and four destroyers coming from Chinese waters. These two groups were supposed to transit Surigao Strait together, but Shima was late as we shall discover.

The North Group, containing the Japanese aircraft carriers, was under the command of Vice Admiral Ozawa. It departed from Japan as scheduled, making its trek toward Luzon, hoping to be discovered by none other than Admiral Halsey.

The Center Force, under Kurita, was first detected by Americans as it sailed through the narrow Palawan Passage in the South China Sea, approaching the Philippines from the west. Our submarines *Darter* and *Dace*, operating in that passage, discovered them shortly after midnight on the 23rd, and immediately radioed the news to our forces. Thus Halsey of the Third Fleet and Kinkaid of the Seventh Fleet were alerted that the Japanese naval forces were en route.

The *Darter* and the *Dace* managed to inflict the first casualties on the Japanese, torpedoing three cruisers. Among these was the *Atago*, flagship of Kurita. Exploding and sinking rapidly, the *Atago* had to be abandoned. Dunked abruptly into the sea, Kurita was fished from the waters and afterwards shifted his flag to the battle-

The USS Samuel B. Roberts (DE-413) leaving the WAYS Brown Shipbuilding Co., Houston, Texas, 20 January 1944.

The USS Samuel B. Roberts (DE-413) in the Philippine Sea. Mid-October 1944. Photo taken from its sister ship, the USS Wann (DE-412) as the two ships were maneuvering to exchange movie films and guard mail. The flag hoist indicates course and speed of the Roberts.

USN/NA 80-G-284450. USS White Plains (CVE-66) bracketed by shellfire as battle begins, as CVE in foreground begins to launch aircraft.

USN/NA 80-G-287426. USS White Plains (CVE-66) in background bracketed by shell fire as foreground CVE continues to launch aircraft. A Japanese cruiser in far background center is firing. CVE on far right is unidentified.

USN/NA 80-G-287457. Destroyer escorts begin making a smoke screen to shield the Jeep carriers, and Japanese salvos land in water nearby.

USN/NA 80-G-288144. Destroyer escorts to the left begin to make a smoke screen to protect USS Gambier Bay (CVE-73) on the right foreground. The CVE is also making smoke.

USN/NA 80-G-287459. USS Dennis (DE-405) belching both black and white smoke for the smoke screen.

USN/NA 80-G-288145. Two destroyer escorts and USS Gambier Bay (CVE-73) making smoke.

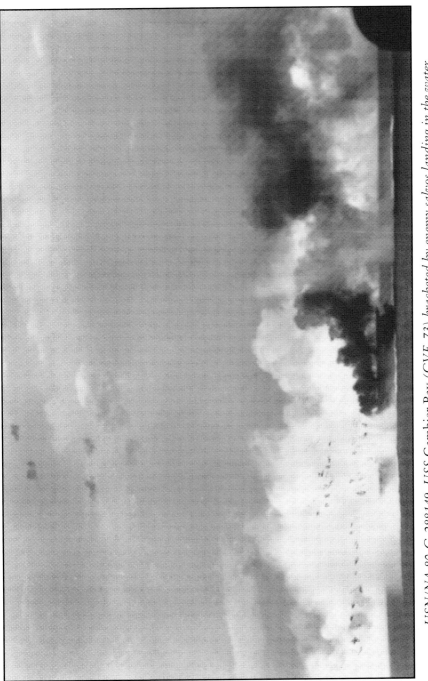

USN/NA 80-G-288149. USS Gambier Bay (CVE-73) bracketed by enemy salvos landing in the water.

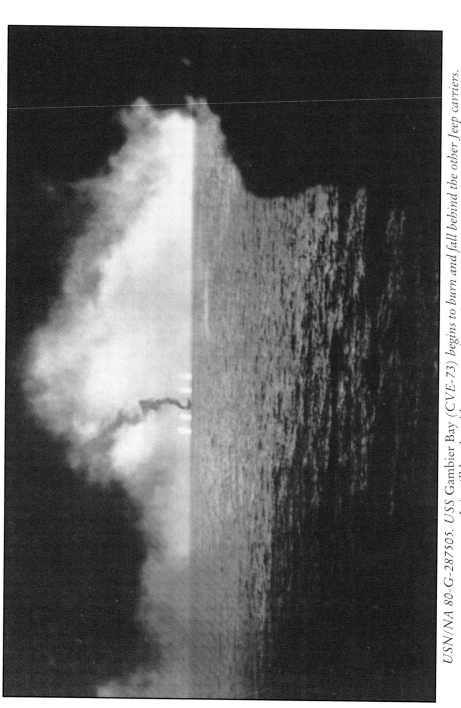

USN/NA 80-G-287505. USS Gambier Bay (CVE-73) begins to burn and fall behind the other Jeep carriers. It is still bracketed by enemy salvos splashing in the sea.

USN/NA 80-G-287512. *Sailors on a Jeep carrier watch as the USS Gambier Bay (CVE-73) falls farther behind. Badly hit by enemy shells its fire has begun to spread. Soon it will be dead in the water and be abandoned.*

USN/NA 80-G-287500. An unidentified Jeep carrier makes smoke as enemy salvos splash nearby in the sea.

USN/NA 80-G-270516. The USS St. Lo (CVE-63) explodes in a massive fireball when struck by a kamikaze plane.

USN/NA 80-G-248122. The USS Hoel (DD-533) in the screen of the Jeep carriers the day before the battle off Samar. This was one of the ships sunk by Kurita's mighty force on 25 October 1944.

USN/NA 80-G-270517. The USS Heermann (DD-532) as the battle off Samar begins. This was the only destroyer that survived, but it was badly damaged.

Two crewmen of a rescue ship pull an oil-soaked survivor of the battle off Samar from the ocean. All survivors were so thoroughly soaked with fuel oil their clothes had to be thrown overboard once they were safely aboard a rescue ship. The fuel oil was something of a blessing, as it tended to keep the sharks away during their fifty hours adrift in the Philippine Sea.

ship *Yamato*. The damage wrought by our two submarines was the opening salvo of a four-day engagement between the Japanese and American fleets, engagements that became known as the Battle of Leyte Gulf.

By virtue of the alert action by the *Darter* and the *Dace*, our naval commanders were ready. Aircraft searches discovered the approach of the South Force and tracked the route of the Center Force.

As this Center Force entered the Sibuyan Sea, approaching San Bernardino Strait, the aircraft from Halsey's huge carriers carried out vicious attacks. Kurita's ships, lacking assistance from any Japanese aircraft, suffered a terrible pounding. Kurita's major losses were a cruiser and a battleship, and he turned back to the west. Our aircraft pilots seem to have exaggerated the damage inflicted on Kurita's ships, for Halsey recalled our aircraft, apparently thinking significant damage had been done to deter that Center Force. After two hours or so, with no more aircraft attacks, Kurita turned east and again began his approach to San Bernardino Strait.

Kinkaid had his Seventh Fleet in Leyte Gulf; Halsey had his Task Force 38 of the Third Fleet off San Bernardino Strait. At this time Halsey sent a radio message to Nimitz that he would form a Task Force 34 of some of his ships. This message was intercepted by Kinkaid. As a result, it was believed by Nimitz at Pearl and Kinkaid of the Seventh Fleet that this new force would guard San Bernardino Strait if Halsey's main force ever departed that area. The failure to be positive (as Halsey, personally, in his own mind, thought it was something he might do only in the future) misled both Nimitz and Kinkaid as to his intentions regarding the use of Task Force 34.

In the meantime, Ozawa, as planned, managed to be "discovered" by Halsey, who promptly fell for the bait. At full speed he steamed north, toward Luzon, with all of his fast carriers, modern battleships, cruisers and destroyers — leaving none behind to guard San Bernardino Strait. He personally felt the Seventh Fleet would take care of that guard duty should the occasion arise. Halsey's message that he was headed north did not state that he was taking *all* of Task Force 38, but rather was worded to indicate three groups of ships. This reinforced the belief in the minds of Kinkaid and Nimitz that such a new Task Force 34 had been formed and was left behind to guard San Bernardino Strait.

Thus, with the discovery of the South Force approaching the Mindano Sea and Surigao Strait, Kincaid moved his battleships, cruisers and most of his destroyers to the extreme south end of the Leyte Gulf area, far away from our main landing areas, so as to meet the enemy fleet as it tried to exit that strait.

As a result of these actions by Halsey and Kinkaid, the only navy ships now located off of the Leyte Gulf landing area were the three groups of Jeep carriers, with their antisubmarine screens composed of a few destroyers and destroyer escorts. Accordingly, as night approached on 24 October, these three small groups, known as Taffy 1, 2 and 3, were our only naval ships anywhere near Samar and the northern entrance to Leyte Gulf. Taffy 3, which contained the *Roberts*, was the most northern group, located off Samar Island, closest to the now unguarded San Bernardino Strait as it enters the Philippine Sea.

With Kurita's formidable group now entering San Bernardino Strait with impunity, the scene was set for its upcoming encounter with Taffy 3 — an encounter which resulted in the heroic action of the men of the *Roberts* and the men of the other small ships of its group.

At dawn, when faulty communications and the lack of a unified command had laid the groundwork for disaster, only unparalleled American guts and gumption would save the day.

8

Leyte: Part II

Admiral Kinkaid, embarked on the command ship, the USS *Wasatch*, placed Rear Adm. Jesse Oldendorf in charge of the combatant ships of the Seventh Fleet that would soon engage the Japanese Southern Force at Surigao Strait. These included six old battleships, eight cruisers, and three squadrons of destroyers. Admiral Oldendorf stationed these ships in battle lines across the exit of Surigao Strait as it enters the extreme southern area of Leyte Gulf.

Further ahead, well into the Mindanao Sea, some PT boats were stationed. They were the first naval elements to make contact with the ships under the command of Admiral Nishimura. This initial encounter by PT boats took place slightly more than an hour before midnight on 24 October. With this contact, radio silence was broken, and voice radio reports and orders ensued. As a result, the men in Taffy 1, 2, and 3 tuned to the battle radio frequencies, becoming aware of the naval battle which began to take shape more than a hundred miles away.

Nishimura had not waited for Admiral Shima's group to join him, but had plodded on ahead. When he departed the Mindanao Sea and entered the narrower waters of Surigao Strait, his ships had to move in column-type formations in order to approach Leyte Gulf. Their ability to maneuver was restricted by this narrow strait. As a result, only their forward mounted guns, generally, could engage the American forces. Oldendorf and his awesome force were lined up abeam the exit of Surigao Strait, so all guns on American ships could fire at the enemy. It was a classic example of the naval maneuver known since the days of Lord Nelson as "crossing the T."

In the face of such withering firepower, Nishimura's group was dealt a crushing defeat. The ships of Admiral Shima, following shortly behind, met the same fate. By about 0400 on the morning of the 25th, the portion of the battle at Surigao Strait was over. Only a few wounded elements of the Japanese fleet were still afloat — barely able to maneuver, desperately seeking to escape.

(In another part of this book are reproductions of maps drawn by the cartographic officer on the USS *Wasatch* depicting the disposition of the various battle groups involved in this mighty naval engagement which raged for over five hours.)

On the *Roberts*, and on the other ships in Taffy 3, the battle at Surigao Strait, as heard on the voice radio, was so exciting that many personnel were up all night listening in awe as events unfolded.

Just before dawn each day, all ships in Taffy 3 went to General Quarters to guard against submarine attacks, which commonly occurred in the haze just before sunrise. At the same time, the Jeep carriers launched a few aircraft to scout for enemy submarines. The morning of 25 October was no exception. With no submarines encountered, the ships secured from General Quarters shortly after sunrise. LCDR Copeland, the skipper of the *Roberts*, in his unpublished reminiscences, related:

> I didn't get any sleep that night because about midnight all hell broke loose on the radios. . . . Our battleships, cruisers and destroyers found the Jap fleet coming into the Gulf via Surigao Strait. . . . Our radio was on a voice frequency and we could hear everyone down there giving their commands and we could hear the heavy guns booming. My Exec and I became so excited that we just camped in CIC until it was time to go up for the pre-dawn flight. . . . It was after the pre-dawn GQ on the morning of 25 October 1944 that our own fireworks really began.

And what fireworks they were! Unbeknownst to the men of Taffy 3, Kurita and his mighty force — which still contained four

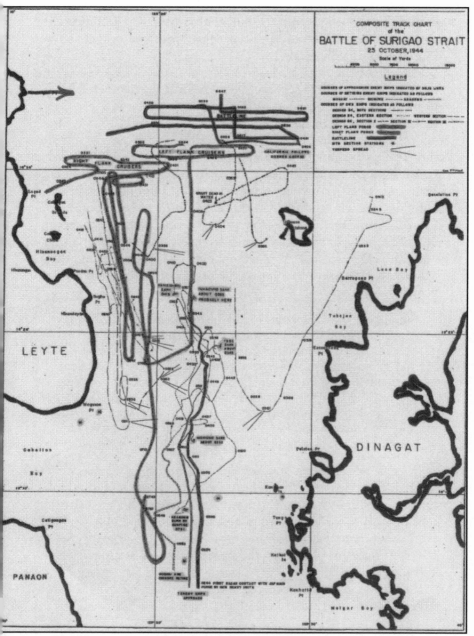

This shows the movements of Seventh Fleet battleships, cruisers, and destroyers that roundly defeated the ships of Nishimura and Shima which entered the narrow strait in column formation. Thus, we crossed the "T."

— Courtesy of H. S. (Gus) Edwards, former cartographic officer.
A copy was furnished to U.S. Naval Historical Center in 1995 by Mr. Edwards.

battleships, six heavy cruisers, one light cruiser, and accompanying destroyers — had cleared San Bernardino Strait undetected and was fast bearing down upon them.

None of the ships in Taffy 3 were at General Quarters at this time. In fact, they had secured from GQ and the men were headed to morning chow. Some ack-ack fire on the horizon to the north caused the watch on the bridge to take notice. At the same time a pilot, by voice radio, reported enemy ships to the north. Initially, this report was thought to be a misidentification. In fact, Rear Adm. C.A.F. Sprague, commander of Taffy 3, ordered the pilot to check again and verify for certain, thinking that the pilot must be in error. How could enemy ships be in this area? Even when the pilot confirmed enemy ships, it was thought that they were wounded elements of the Japanese ships fleeing from the night battle at Surigao Strait. LCDR Copeland, who was on his way from the bridge of the *Roberts* to get a cup of coffee in the wardroom, recalled what happened:

> I heard one of the lookouts call to the officer of the deck, "object on the horizon, looks like the mast of a ship." One of the last things I had heard during the night on the combat radio frequency was that our ships had routed the Jap fleet . . . they were talking back and forth in plain English how they were chasing the fleeing remnants. . . . So we were lulled into a false sense of security. . . . Now we didn't know which way our fleet was chasing the Japs . . . whether some had broken through, or out to sea, or where they were.

As on some other units of Taffy 3, once pagoda masts were sighted, the ships were thought, initially, to be wounded cripples. On several ships in Taffy 3, the word was passed for men to come topside if they wished to see fleeing enemy ships. Suddenly, however, salvos whistled overhead and began to splash nearby in the water. At that, one old salt on the signal bridge was heard to exclaim, "Fleeing, my ass!"

John Maco, fireman 3rd class, from Syracuse, New York, wrote to me:

> It was roughly 0645 or 0650 on 25 October and we were getting ready for breakfast . . . [there was] an anouncement on the PA system that if anyone would like to see enemy ships they could look astern. I looked and there they were. I counted 24 masts

across the horizon. In a matter of a minute or two, shells began falling in the water . . . general quarters was sounded. . . . I made my way to the forward 20mm gun mount, my GQ station.

Whitney Felt, sonar man 3rd class, similarly recalled:

I had the 0400 to 0800 watch the morning of 25 October . . . rotating between the Sound Hut, CIC and the Bridge. . . . I remember being surprised when the chief quartermaster, Frank Cantrell, came up on the bridge after we had secured from dawn GQ, glanced at accompaning ships through the long-glass, then turned his attention astern. I remember seeing him brace his legs, steady the telescope with a stanchion, and shake his head. . . . Frank called over the intercom, "Mr. Roberts (the executive officer), please come to the bridge" . . . . When the Exec appeared, Frank asked him if he had ever seen a Japanese ship. "No," the Exec admitted, "but I have seen silhouettes of them. Why?" Frank directed his attention to the tiny specs on the horizon. . . . "By God!" Mr. Roberts exclaimed after looking through the glass, "Those ships certainly have pagoda superstructures!" . . . . The Exec called the skipper, and after they and Frank conferred, the Exec went to the intercom and said: "This is Mr. Roberts. When you men finish your breakfast and before you relieve the watch, you might want to go aft on the boat deck and look astern. You'll see some remnants of the Japanese fleet which are fleeing." I continued to look astern and the dots were now quite visible to the naked eye. Why, I wondered, if the ships were fleeing, were they getting larger? Shipmates headed for the boat deck, and those with bridge privileges came up to look at the Japanese fleet. Suddenly there were white puffs of smoke visible from the enemy ships, and moments later I could hear a whistling sound I'd never heard before, and almost immediately there were hugh splashes nearby in the water, strangely colored green and blue and yellow. The captain hit the GQ alarm, pulled down the TBS (voice radio between ships) microphone which was only used in most dire circumstances, and alerted Admiral Sprague: "This is Juggernaut. We are being fired upon. I repeat, we are being fired upon!" I headed for the sound hut, my GQ station, and put on my Mae West life jacket and crash helmet.

Once the salvos commenced, all ships went to General Quarters, and soon the extent of the enemy force became apparent. The heavily armored Japanese ships, many able to withstand hits by the largest guns of any naval ship in our fleet, were opposed by only three destroyers, four destroyer escorts, and six little Jeep carriers. These were the only ships standing in the way of the entrance to Leyte Gulf and our supply ships unloading in that area, as well as our troops already ashore. These small American ships had no armor plating, absolutely nothing to withstand hits by any of the enemy guns. As for armament, the largest guns on the ships in Taffy 3 were 5-inch/38 types. On the other hand, the Japanese ships had guns ranging up to 18.1 inches — the largest naval guns ever built. It was a case of "pea-shooters" against "Big Berthas," or a high school football team versus the Dallas Cowboys! A disastrously mismatched Super Bowl was in the offing.

In the face of such overwhelming odds, and realizing the perilous situation facing them and our troops ashore, the men of Taffy 3 dug in their heels and made the equivalent of a high school Friday night "goal line stand." Their many practice drills served them well, as each ship went about its maneuvers to distract and harass the enemy. The calm and professional manner in which the officers and crews conducted themselves, in a seemingly hopeless situation, is vivid testimony to the spunk and guts of Americans in a crisis situation.

Thomas J. Stevenson, Jr., of Tobyhanna, Pennsylvania, then a lieutenant (jg), wrote to me:

> I was on watch during the night of 24 October in the Combat Information Center (CIC), and was able to hear some of the events of the battle at Surigao Strait, as many of the TBS broadcasts were skipping as they frequently did in those latitudes. The morning of 25 October I went back to the "sack" after dawn GQ. I had a skivvy shirt and khaki trousers on and was dozing when the Exec came on the squark box and announced that the remnants of the Japanese fleet from the battle were fleeing over the horizon and if we came on deck we could see the pagoda masts. I slipped on a pair of bedroom slippers and went up on deck. When I looked out I could see, very vaguely, the masts of some ships; but immediately I also saw colored shell bursts all around us and heard the General Quarters Alarm. I ran to my station which was in CIC, where I was the assistant plotting officer. When I arrived at CIC, I could see the size of the Japanese fleet on the radar screen and realized only too well what we were up against.

This was typical of the responses I have received from many survivors of the *Roberts*. Lt. (jg) Stevenson began his assigned duties just as he had done many times before in numerous practice drills since the ship had departed Texas waters some six months earlier. Other members of ship's company, in various stages of dress and undress, did likewise; some were barefoot, some wet from a shower, as all hands reported to their GQ stations on the double. The emergency was too great to delay for even a moment.

En route to CIC, Tom Stevenson crossed paths with Ens. John S. LeClercq, who was going from the bridge area of the ship to the director for the aft 40mm gun. As Stevenson wrote, a month later, to the parents of LeClercq:

> [Glancing at the ships on the horizon] John and I saw there was little chance of survival, so we shook hands and wished each other luck before continuing to our respective battle stations.

James F. (Bud) Comet was a nineteen-year-old seaman, assigned to the Gunnery Division on the *Roberts*, and John LeClercq was his division officer. Bud, in a lengthy telephone interview, told me that when GQ sounded he was on watch at the aft 40mm gun, while his GQ station was on the forward 40mm gun. As Bud came down the ladder from his watch station to the main deck, he met John LeClercq ready to climb that ladder. Exchanging salutes, each said, "Good morning." As John began to climb, he looked back at Bud and nonchalantly said: "Do you think the rain will hurt the rhubarb?" Bud explained that John used this phrase whenever danger approached; that it is an expression used in many southern and midwestern rural farming areas when some major problem arises. This attitude seems to have been typical of the almost routine and unperturbed manner in which everyone on the *Roberts*, from the skipper on down, went about their duties in this most perilous situation. Never having been in battle before, on a ship not designed to be in such a battle, they performed as seasoned seamen.

With the realization that this small Task Unit was under attack by an overwhelming force of Japanese ships, Admiral Sprague sent a frantic, plain English, radio message for help from any source, stating his exact position. Unfortunately, any meaningful help was too far away. Halsey, chasing the "bait," was some 200 miles to the north with his modern carriers, fast battleships, and cruisers. Kinkaid's combat ships were some 100 miles to the south. Taffy 2 was about 30 miles to the south, and it prepared to send its planes. However, as with the planes in Taffy 3, the largest bomb that they could carry was a 500-pound SAP — too small to inflict more than harassment and minor damage on the heavily armored capital ships.

That radio message alerted everyone to the peril at hand. At Pearl Harbor, Admiral Nimitz and his staff realized only too well the apparent tragedy that was imminent. So did the brass in Washington, D.C. Both now realized Halsey's Task Force 34 had not been guarding the area where San Bernardino Strait enters the Philippine Sea. It was "nail biting" time for the high commands in both Hawaii and Washington.

But Admiral Sprague never flinched. To give his little carriers time to launch their aircraft, he promptly ordered the destroyers and destroyer escorts to "make smoke" between the enemy ships and his carriers. The log book of the USS *Dennis* (DE-405) reflects that at 0705 the smoke screen operation commenced. Heavy black and white smoke belched forth from the escorts, making it difficult for the spotters on the enemy ships to properly gauge distance to the carriers. Of course, this made the escorts sitting ducks for an enemy still too far out of the range of American guns. At this time, only our planes, launched from the Jeep carriers, could harass the enemy; and they began to do so in earnest, dropping anything they had, even harmless depth charges! They tried anything to distract and confuse the Japanese.

A narrative by Capt. W.V.R. Vieweg USN, skipper of the *Gambier Bay*, recorded on 18 December 1944 in the Office of Naval Records and Library, indicates that there was a distinct problem launching fully loaded planes due to the lack of sufficient wind over the flight deck. Without permission, he immediately began to launch the aircraft already positioned on the flight deck as soon as contact with the enemy occurred. One torpedo plane with only 35 gallons of gasoline was launched. It did make a successful torpedo run, but with so little fuel, the pilot and plane ditched in the sea and were lost. The battle log, as reconstructed and prepared on 3 November 1944 by Lt. William F. Cordner, aviation ordnance officer, reflects that this heroic pilot was Ens. William Gallagher.

A brief ten-minute rain squall provided some help, especially for the Jeep carriers, since our ships were temporarily well-hidden from visual observation. When this short squall ended, Sprague's units were once again in clear weather and Japanese shellfire resumed in earnest.

Likewise, the destroyers and destroyer escorts resumed their

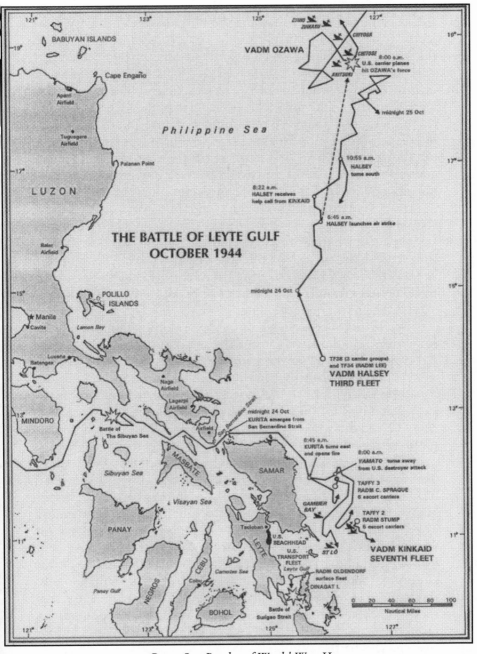

Great Sea Battles of World War II
Reprinted from *Naval History* with permission
Copyright 1995 U.S. Naval Institute

smoke screen operations, dashing about in a frenzy of activity in the face of a maelstrom of enemy gunfire. As a result, in a wild melee in the smoky haze, during which two of our ships missed colliding by only inches, the escorts "chased salvos." This means a ship would race to the spot where a salvo had just landed. The colored dye marker splashes in the sea told the enemy spotters whether a salvo had been short or long, and their gunners would immediately crank in a distance correction for the next salvo. But, of course, the American ship would then be located where the previous salvo had landed, and as a result, the new salvo would be wide of its mark. This gave our ships a limited respite, initially providing some protection.

As more Japanese ships began to aim for a particular American ship, this maneuver was not totally effective; soon hits were scored. In fact, enemy gunners began to score significant hits, not only on the escort ships, but also on the little carriers. The log book of each surviving carrier records shellfire damage, even though the armor-piercing shells from the large enemy ships passed through our thin-skinned ships without exploding.

While these shells passed through the ships without exploding, sometimes they did cause damage and an occasional casualty. Percell L. Worley, now of Hanover, Pennsylvania, and who was a machinist's mate on the *Dennis*, reported to me that at the time of this battle, he was on duty in the forward mess hall, manning the battle phone circuit of his ship. In such enclosed quarters, below the main deck, he could not see anything of the battle. However, he vividly recalls that suddenly an 8-inch armor-piercing enemy shell burst through the port side of the hull of his compartment, whizzed by, barely missing him, traveled through a portion of the chief's quarters, and exited the starboard side of the ship just above the water-line. A fellow shipmate in this compartment was the only human casualty from this shell. However, the gaping hole, just above the waterline, allowed sea water to enter the ship each time a wave came by. As a result, the *Dennis* suffered serious flooding in one nearby storeroom and ammunition storage compartment. Undoubtedly, this same scenario was repeated on the other ships of Taffy 3. If these had been high-explosive shells which detonate upon impact, rather than armor-piercing shells, few ships of Taffy 3 would have survived this battle.

In addition the enemy launched torpedo attacks at the escorts, without scoring any hits. On the *Roberts*, the 40mm guns were used to shoot at approaching torpedoes, particularly the aft 40mm gun under the control of John LeClercq. Fortunately, many Japanese torpedoes were set at a depth to injure very large ships, such as cruisers, and thus passed harmlessly under the shallow draft escorts.

It was then that Admiral Sprague ordered: "Wolves, make a torpedo attack." The term "wolves" was the voice radio call signal for the destroyers. The *Roberts* was then near the three destroyers, and inquired by radio as to whether "little wolves," by which the destroyer escorts were known, should participate. Finally receiving an affirmative response from the admiral, the *Roberts* made its own torpedo run following along behind the three destroyers. It launched its two torpedoes under most trying conditions, during which an enemy shellburst in the aft 40mm gun mount area killed John LeClercq and nearly everyone topside who was nearby. The damage resulting from this shellburst hampered the operation of gun 52. The *Roberts* scored a torpedo hit on one cruiser, after bravely closing range to about 2,500 yards. One survivor told me that they were so close to the cruiser that the large 8-inch guns of the cruiser could not be trained low enough to shoot a small ship at such close range. As it closed the range for this torpedo run, the *Roberts* was finally able to use its two 5-inch/38 guns effectively on more than one enemy ship.

Retiring from this run, the *Roberts* took serious hits from another enemy ship that had it in their sights. Some shells passed through the thin-skinned hulls of the *Roberts*, as they did in other ships of Taffy 3, without serious damage. These were armor-piercing shells, which would not explode immediately upon hitting a target, but were designed to burst once they passed though heavy armor plate. The Japanese had fired some such shells, in the mistaken belief they were dealing with capital ships of the American fleet. In interrogations at Tokyo after the war, it was discovered that the Japanese recognition officers initially had classified the *Roberts* and its fellow escorts as American cruisers! To make such a serious mistake, they must have had very meager training for ship recognition. Thus, in many instances, the Japanese mistakenly used armor-piercing shells rather than high-explosive shells.

As Lt. E. E. Roberts, Jr., now of Moorestown, New Jersey, whose GQ station was in CIC as plotting officer, wrote:

The captain ordered a torpedo attack. I computed the course to bring us within launch range. My hands were ice cold from fear. I wished he had ordered me to find a course that would be an escape route. We launched the torpedos and fired our 5-inch guns at a very close range. Finally they started to hit us with their shells. The large shells (armor piercing) went through the hull without detonating, but a salvo of 5-inch shells in the engineering spaces stopped us dead in the water. The CIC room became full of asbestos from the insulation being jarred off the piping. It became clear that the ship was sinking.

These hits in the engineering spaces of the *Roberts* tore open the steam lines, and scalding water poured out on the men of the engineering gang, killing most of them. Now, with the *Roberts* dead in the water and sinking, at 0910, after more than a two-hour running battle, LCDR Copeland, the captain, gave the order to abandon ship.

The real ordeal for the men of the *Roberts* was at hand.

9

Survival at Sea: Part I

The *Roberts* was not the first ship which had to be abandoned. Like the *Roberts*, the three destroyers, *Hoel*, *Johnston*, and *Heermann*, which had led that torpedo run, received a terrible pummeling from Japanese gunfire as they closed in on several enemy cruisers. This magnified the damage already sustained by these four ships during the past two hours. At 0840 the *Hoel*, which had led the torpedo charge, was abandoned just in time, for at 0855 she rolled over on her port side and sank, stern first. At 0945, with her superstructure in utter shambles, the *Johnston* also was abandoned. She rolled over and sank at 1010, taking her mortally wounded Cherokee skipper, Cdr. Ernest E. Evans, with her. The *Heermann*, badly wounded, managed to limp away.

Among the Jeep carriers, the *Gambier Bay*, having earlier received severe damage in its engineering spaces, fell behind the other carriers. According to the narrative of Captain Vieweg, the *Gambier Bay* took a hit almost every other minute. Some shells caused small fires which were quickly suppressed, as long as there was water pressure for the fire hoses. However, when both engine rooms became flooded, all water pressure was lost; then small fires quickly became

roaring fires. Thereupon, badly damaged, dead in the water, and falling prey to several Japanese ships which closed in for the kill, the
Gambier Bay began to sink rapidly. Captain Vieweg gave the order
to abandon ship. Some rafts were thrown overboard. As there was
precious little time to escape, undoubtedly many, like Captain Vieweg, jumped into the sea. He recalled that only moments after he
was in the water the ship rolled over about 0904, and quickly sank.
The subsequent ordeal of its personnel was much the same as that of
the men from the *Roberts*.

Various survivors of the *Roberts* have given me vivid accounts
of the subsequent events which they encountered and their heroic
struggle to survive at sea. Their own words best relate what occurred.

When a navy ship is to be abandoned, steps must be taken to
ensure that the decoding machine (ECM) is destroyed, along with
all of the secret and top secret publications. Wounded personnel
must be assisted as all hands take to the life rafts and floater nets
which are used in such an emergency.

Lt. (jg) Tom Stevenson, who was the communications officer,
gave me an excellent account of the final moments aboard ship and
the subsequent hardships endured for over fifty hours by the men
on the nets and rafts:

> After the torpedo attack . . . the ship took a hit in the #1 fire
> room which was directly below and slighty aft of the CIC and the
> Radio Shack. The steam from the ruptured steam lines flooded up
> into those two stations, driving all of us therefrom. Some of the
> men went down on the main deck where several of them, includ-
> ing Chief Radioman Serrafini and Dick Rohde, RM3c, were seri-
> ously wounded (from burns and shrapnel). . . . I ran up on the
> bridge which was quite crowded with refugees from the lower
> deck, then to the signal bridge. . . . A shell hit just aft of that area
> and we were knocked down by the concussion; the flags bags went
> on fire. . . . By this time we were operating at half power and it
> appeared we were going to be OK. . . . We were firing all out at a
> cruiser when we took several quick hits and lost all power. John
> LeClercq's battle station and the aft end of the housing disap-
> peared and the ship went dead in the water.
>
> My recollection is that the captain then ordered: "Carry out
> the Destruction Bill, scuttle and abandon ship." The Destruction
> Bill involved me to a great extent. I went down to the Radio Shack
> and threw the wheels to the secret Electric Coding Machine

This is a replica of the original painting of the sinking of the USS Gambier Bay (CVE-73), entitled "Freedom's Cost," which now hangs in the Franklin Delano Roosevelt Presidential Library at Hyde Park, New York.

(ECM) overboard. We had been trained in Communication School that the ECM and all of its wheels had to be destroyed if there was any danger of them falling into enemy hands; else we were better off to go down with the ship. I was supposed to have a hand grenade lodged in the side of the machine in the event of destruction being required; but I never put one in the receptacle thinking that "this could never happen," as well as fearing I might accidently blow myself up. A sonarman named Cayo had a submachine gun and he sprayed the ECM for me and did an effective job.

The captain then reminded me to destroy all of the secret publications, including the invasion plans, as he was fearful the Japanese would board the vessel if, by chance, she did not sink quickly. The safe with all those documents was below decks, next to my room. . . . I enlisted the aid of Joe Nabors, a signalman striker, to go down through the scuttle with me to help carry the weighted bags once I opened the safe. With shaking fingers I managed to open the safe; the ship was listing badly and the space was dimly lighted as only the emergency battle lights (on batteries) were functioning. He and I took the weighted bags up on deck and threw them overboard, but there were too many bags for one trip. Nabors decided he did not want to go back down below again, so I went alone. This time I grabbed a life preserver from my room, but was so anxious to get out of there, I neglected to take my wallet and college ring. By this time I thought most everyone (who was able) had left the ship, except the captain and first lieutenant. Then Chief Machinist Mate Charles Smith crawled out of the engine room and was dying and begging to be put in the water. We gave him a shot of morphine and put him in the water. I jumped in . . . and struck out for a raft several hundred yards out. When I reached the raft there were about forty men on it and a floater net. . . . A large Japanese ship steamed by us and it appeared they were taking moving pictures of us. . . .

After a short time a Navy plane flew over us quite low and waggled its wings; so we thought we would be picked up right away. The day wore on and the only planes we saw were very high and evidently not looking for us; even so, we spread some orange dye from the raft, but to no avail. We saw some of our men on some scaffolding or planking several hundred yards away, and Lt. Gurnett and I swam to them. We took a badly wounded man back with us to our raft; the others would not come. During the night we heard someone calling and we called back. It was Cayo, and he joined us. He had been on the planking and they had been attacked by sharks. Only he survived.

On the second day our morale was going down, so I thought we would be better off doing something rather than just waiting and hoping. There were two paddles on the raft, and, using them, we attempted to go towards Samar, but to no avail. The paddling exhausted us. During our paddling, a sea gull started circling us, and Cayo, envisioning a hearty raw meal, swung his paddle at it. Missing the gull, he accidently hit me over the head, almost knocking me unconscious. I lost my head and went after him, not realizing what he was doing. We had begun to lose our sense of tolerance of each other, and it was starting to be every man for himself; although there were many instances of shipmates helping each other in acts of unselfish courage. I, myself, was a beneficiary of such an act. I had begun to hallucinate during the second night as a result of drinking some salt water, and I either lost consciousness or fell asleep due to overexertion trying to paddle the raft. I was in the water, hanging on to the floater net, and I had a life belt rather than a Mae West which would have kept my head out of the water. Mr. Gurnett and Mr. Roberts took turns holding my head up out of the water; else I would not have survived.

The next day we were sighted by a small group of ships which thought we were Jap submarines. They approached us and we could see the American flags. An LCI pulled up to us with their guns trained on us, and we shouted we were Americans. Since we were covered with fuel oil we looked like Japs to them. On a bull horn, they asked who won the world series (which had just ended). Someone gave the correct answer so they picked us out of the water; most of us by use of stretchers. We were so filthy that the crew turned a hose on us to try and wash off some of the oil.

Chief Serafini had given me his wallet when he was on the raft and asked me to give it to his wife. He did not think he would make it due to his serious leg wounds. When he was laying*[sic]* on deck in a wire basket stretcher I gave him back his wallet, saying: "Tullio, you made it!" He was placed in the captain's cabin and we sailed for Leyte Gulf. The next morning when we arrived at anchorage, he was dead; but his wallet was missing.

In that same raft group with Lt. (jg)Tom Stevenson, were LCDR Copeland, Lieutenants Roberts, Burton, Gurnett, and Ensign Moylan, as well as nearly forty members of the crew. The two engineering officers, Lieutenant Trowbridge and Ensign Riebenbauer, and the gunnery officer, Lieutenant (jg) LeClercq, had been killed in action and went down with the ship. Drifting separately on another group of rafts with about seventy-six men were Ensign

Moore and Ensign West. The ordeal of that group appears in a detailed narrative set forth in Chapter 10.

Lieutenant Roberts, the executive officer, related matters similar to those of Tom Stevenson. However, he noted that they were continually in a large patch of fuel oil from their ship, which oil floated along with the raft. While it seriously bothered everyone's eyes, it proved to be a blessing for it provided some protection from the blistering tropical sun, and it tended to keep the sharks away. He reported:

> There were sharks around us, but they kept clear of the oil patch. One sailor, being fastidious and regular, swam away from the group, out of the oil patch, to defecate. When he lowered his pants a shark nudged him. Quickly he scrambled back to the group in the oil patch.
>
> Hallucinations, due to sun, exposure, and fatigue, were common. An officer swam up to me, saluted, and requested "permission to go below." I gave it, and he swam away. . . .
>
> During the night, in my own hallucination, I "saw" we were being swept by the current past a point of land on which there were lovely homes. There was a gala dinner party taking place in one of them. The men wore tuxes and the ladies wore beautiful gowns. . . . Daybreak brought me back to reality.
>
> [Then] I tried to bargain with God. I explained to him that my wife had just had a baby boy whom I had never seen, and that though I was ready and willing to die, if HE would allow it I would take care of them as long as I lived. . . .
>
> The morning of the third day we could see land on the horizon. We assumed the Japanese had wiped out General MacArthur's landing forces and were in control of the island, so we made plans to sneak ashore and find some friendly forces. . . . A little later we then sighted some ships on the horizon [the rescue ships].

Ensign Moylan, the officer of the deck at General Quarters, had a good view of everything that occurred during the battle. He vividly recalled that the enormous flames on the *Gambier Bay* were unnerving, but seeing close-up the destruction on the *Hoel* and the *Johnston* was even more disturbing. He remembered only too well the shellburst that destroyed LeClercq's station, because it knocked everyone who was on the open bridge to the deck. Later, during the second day of clinging to the raft, he tied himself to it since he realized he could not hold on much longer. He was told that he only survived because a sailor held his head out of the water. At the moment of rescue he was unconscious and in such poor physical condition that the crew of the rescue ship had to haul him aboard. He did not regain consciousness until he was on a hospital ship.

Louis Gould, who was a sonarman 3rd class, was in the sound hut operating the sonar gear during General Quarters. With the guns of the *Roberts* firing, and the ship taking hits from enemy ships, the sound gear ceased functioning. He then walked out on the open bridge to watch events unfold. When that shellburst hit the fireroom and steam began rising into CIC and the radio shack, he recalls it became very, very hot on the bridge. When the order was given to abandon ship, he and Cayo, a fellow sonarman, smashed the tubes on the sonar gear, and Cayo, who had a submachine gun, began firing at the equipment. He said: "Bullets flew all over the place, but luckily we were not hit." His experiences on the raft with the captain were similar to those already related.

Wayne Moses, a gunner's mate striker, went over the starboard side of the ship when the order was given to abandon ship. He wrote in a letter to me:

> I had no life jacket . . . a sailor swam to me and helped put a Mae West on me, and helped me get to the raft and net where Captain Copeland was. . . . [During the hours at the raft] I thought of my mother, father and my 15 brothers and sisters, and in my mind I was saying goodbye. . . . I got shook up when some of my buddies*[sic]* nerves gave way from pain and burns, and I could do nothing to help. A couple of men went out of their head, said they were going on watch, jumped off the raft and I never saw them again . . . the oil soaked our skin; we burned by day; at night the cold ocean was more than one can take.

Whit Felt, in his report, mentioned the terrible suffering which was endured, especially by the most seriously wounded. There was no way to ease the pain of the dying men. Among other things, he told me:

> During the day two men died from the wounds they suffered, and we removed their dog tags and pushed them away from the net. One floated near us for an hour or two, and it seemed as if he was an outcast who wanted to rejoin the group. He finally drifted away. . . . The nights were endless. We couldn't sleep. With our arms interlocked we felt if we fell asleep and drifted away, the

other would awaken, and this worked fairly well. Two or three times during the night Vince [Goodrich] grabbed hold of me and pulled me back onto the net, and I did the same for him. A number of other men weren't that fortunate, and several who were on the net at dusk had disappeared by morning. It was ghastly. . . . Everyone was exhausted and [wounded] men [suffering excruciating pain] cried out for their wives or mothers, while others burst into tears and sobbed like childern. . . . I had a number of horrible dreams.

Mel Harden, a seaman in the Deck Division, was the hot shell-man on the forward 5-inch/38 gun at General Quarters. He was on watch at the time of the encounter with Kurita's ships. In a very detailed letter he mentioned that his gun crew had to hold their fire until the *Roberts* closed range on enemy ships. When they were finally able to commence firing, the range was so close that their gun barrel was pointed straight out. As he recalled:

At one point the ship suddenly shuddered violently, and everyone that was standing found themselves in a heap on the deck. . . . Sometime during this time an eight inch shell went through our lower magazine, entering above the waterline and exiting below the waterline. This caused the magazine to flood, but not before all remaining ammo was passed up to the next level . . . (taking hits) the front of our gun mount on the port side disintegrated . . . and some of us received minor shrapnel wounds. I lost a dog tag when a piece of shrapnel cut off the small chain as it hung outside of my shirt. . . . My abandon ship station was #1 raft, forward, starboard side. . . . When the raft was cut loose it fell in the water, as did a cork net . . . people began jumping [into the water] or climbing down a cargo net onto the raft and net. . . . When we got about even with the aft 5-inch gun we could see the damage to that gun and the spot where the aft 40mm gun and gun director had been. The entire aft part of the superstructure was completely blown away. We could see bodies on the deck, but there was no movement . . . seeing no movement we paddled away from the ship. . . . About 300 yards away we met up with a cork net containing Captain Copeland, several other officers and men, and tied all nets and the raft together. The captain ordered the most severely wounded be put upon the raft; the others of us got on the net or tied ourselves to the raft. . . . I don't recall how long we were in the water before our ship went down. We watched as she began to roll to port, then she stood straight up with bow in the air, and then slid straight down until it disappeared . . . then three Jap ships headed in our direction. . . . As they went by some Japs were taking pictures, some saluted us, and some appeared to be celebrating. . . . A little while later we watched [in amazement] as the entire Jap force changed course and sailed away! . . . A couple of our planes flew by us, wagged their wings, and we figured help would soon be on its way. By late afternoon, no help having arrived, the captain broke out the emergency rations . . . having had no food since the previous night, we were hungry. . . . As we filed past the raft, the captain and the exec would drop something in our mouth. We got one salt tablet, a piece of spam or hardtack, and a very small drink of water with which to wash down this "feast." We then drifted into a very large patch of very thick fuel oil and became coated with this foul smelling goop . . . this goop protected us from sharks and kept the sun from burning us. . . . The next day we had drifted near Samar, and everyone began to paddle, to no avail. . . . After dark we saw some lights ashore, and Chambless, our first class signalman, tried to communicate with someone, using our little floater light, but had no response. . . .

I imagine it was early afternoon the third day when a ship was sighted, an LCI. After a lot of shouting and waving it headed our way, but with guns pointed . . . asking questions and getting answers only a US Navy man could give [re: the World Series], they took us aboard. . . .

Some other survivors that had earlier been picked up were on deck cleaning themselves, and we joined them. More cleaner was brought on deck, and like those other survivors, we stripped off our soggy, oily clothes, [threw them overboard] and began cleaning up. . . . Falling asleep, I woke up the next morning and we began the transfer to other ships. . . . The most seriously wounded went to a hospital ship, the rest of us to some type of command ship . . . [no clothing having been available] I remember very distinctly walking up the ladder to that ship, still stark naked. A CPO took me below, gave me a bar of salt water soap, put me in a shower, and then gave me a pair of pajamas [the only clothing available]. . . . Later that afternoon we were transferred to an LST, given a good meal, a ditty bag and some clothing. . . . Shortly we were en route to Hollandia.

Richard R. Rohde, a radioman 3rd class, who ended up on the other raft group with Ensign Moore, confirmed much of what I have previously set forth. He was on duty in the radio shack the morning they encountered Kurita. He vividly recalled copying the frantic message for help transmitted by Admiral Sprague. He said that it was the only "plain English" message he ever received while on duty, and that it was sent manually, which made it hard to copy. Rohde quickly realized that they were in for a lot of trouble. As with Mel Harden, he recalled the terrible condition of their clothing from the fuel oil, and the lack of replacement clothing on the rescue ships. After being hosed down along with the others, exhausted from the ordeal at sea, he finally fell into a deep sleep. He said:

> [Before falling asleep], I was given a bowl of oatmeal, which to this day never tasted so good. I, also, received a shot of (medicinal) Canadian Club, and then was laid to rest on the deck of the ship. There was no room below. Since I was not wearing any clothes, and since I happened to wind up over the engine room, to this day I have a burn on my rear end which matches the rivet of the deck plate upon which I was lying.

Thus, Rohde appears to be the only member of ship's company of the *Roberts* who has a visible brand from this ordeal. Undoubtedly, others have invisible, psychological brands which they still carry to this day.

The skipper, LCDR Copeland, in his unpublished manuscript, related the details concerning the heroic action of Paul Henry Carr, gunners mate 3rd class. Carr was the gun captain on the aft 5-inch/38 gun, known as gun 52. During the battle, it had kept firing, even when enemy shells had caused serious mechanical problems in the gun mount and the ammunition hoist from the magazines. When Goheen, a petty officer, went to check on that gun mount, just prior to abandoning ship, he discovered what had occurred. As the skipper related:

> Goheen had to go across a deck covered with burning oil. He went into the gun mount and found a very pathetic condition there. A lot of the men had been completely obliterated . . . what had happened was this: The gun had fired roughly over 300 rounds when, because of hits, it no longer had any power ramming so the men had to ram by hand. Then at the last seven or eight shots the air injection system went out, and the gun was so hot that apparently the 324th round "cooked off" before the automatic breech was completely closed, blew the breech off the gun and the rear end out of the gun mount, and killed most of the men. When Goheen got in there he found Carr, who was ripped clear from his neck to

his groin. He had an eighty-four-pound projecticle in his arms and begged Goheen to help him load it and get it off. He didn't realize that the gun was incapable of firing, and he was still so devoted to duty that he wanted to load the gun. Goheen took it away from him and laid him down. . . . [Goheen then assisted another badly wounded man] . . . went back [in the gun mount]. Carr had gotten that shell again and was trying to load it! Goheen picked up Carr, carried him out, and Carr died there on deck. Carr really spark-plugged that gun crew, and we have recommended him for a post-humous award.

The navy awarded the Silver Star Medal, posthumously, to Paul Henry Carr, and the citation accompanying this award appears in the appendix.

A contemporary recapitulation of the events which occurred on the *Roberts* that fateful day, 25 October 1944, off Samar, and the subsequent ordeal of survival at sea, recently uncovered in my research, appears in the next chapter.

10

Survival at Sea: Part II

The other raft and net group of survivors from the *Roberts* were more numerous. They consisted of about eighty men and Ensigns Moore and West, the two most junior officers on the ship. Survivors from this group have related to me events very similar to information which is described in the previous chapter.

Ed Wheaton, at age twenty-six, was one of the older men serving on the *Roberts* that fateful day in October. Having made a perfect score on the examination at his recruiting station at Sandusky, Ohio, he had his pick of navy schools. Choosing Radio School, he made excellent grades and, upon graduation, became a radio technician, 2nd class. Shortly after arriving on board the *Roberts*, he was advanced to 1st class. Accordingly, his battle station was the radio transmitter room of the radio shack, nearby CIC. When the barrage of enemy shells hit the engineering spaces and wiped out the aft 40mm gun and director, the white paint and asbestos insulation, jarred off the piping in his battle station, completely covered Wheaton. As he went out on deck he saw the skipper, who jokingly remarked to another officer, even under these most trying circumstances: "Look at Wheaton, he looks like Santa Claus!" Immediately thereafter abandon ship was ordered, and he went over the port side of the ship into the water. Aided by Bud Comet, he swam to a raft with Chief Wallace on it. Thus, he became one of that larger group of survivors who, some fifty hours later, were picked up by the USS *PC-623*.

While they, like the men from the other raft, had to throw their oily clothing overboard, Wheaton was lucky enough to be given a pair of surplus dungarees. They had been much too large for anyone on the ship to wear, and they were several sizes too large for him. But he was glad to have anything, and, in a makeshift arrangement, folded them over and tied them around his waist with binder twine. His leg had been injured in the shellfire; thus, upon rescue, he was first transferred to a hospital ship for a day before going on to Hollandia.

Bud Comet, the nineteen-year-old seaman who last saw John LeClercq as they went to their respective battle stations, gave me a very detailed interview by telephone. Since his GQ station was on the forward 40mm gun, he was at the bow area of the ship when the captain gave the order to abandon ship. Most everyone had already jumped into the water on the starboard side of the ship by the time Bud managed to cut loose and lower a raft located on the port side of the ship, forward. He, alone, got on this raft. As it drifted down the port side of the ship, he passed the gaping hole made by the shells which had struck the engineering areas. The raft drifted into that hole and there Bud discoved Cullen Wallace, the ship's chief boatswain mate, standing on the edge of a shattered deck below the main deck, yelling for help. Bud manuevered the raft alongside the deck area and took the chief on board. Wallace had been on a ship which had been sunk earlier at Guadalcanal, and, at first, did not want to take anyone else aboard this raft since its survival rations might be meager. Seeing others in the water, he relented, and aided in their rescue.

As they drifted a short distance astern of the sinking *Roberts*, Bud Comet noticed a young ensign on the stern of the ship, yelling not to be left behind. He was the young supply officer, Jack Moore, who, at age twenty-one, had reported on board for duty only thirty days earlier, fresh out of a brief navy school for supply officers. Everyone else was already in the water. Apparently Moore was actually the last person to leave the ship; at least that was Bud's belief. Moore had gone about the decks checking areas for wounded men and suddenly realized everyone else who was able had already abandoned the ship. Upon hearing Ensign Moore's yell for help, Bud jumped off the raft and plunged into the water. He found a large piece of wooden planking floating nearby and pushed it along in the water toward Moore, who had jumped in the sea and was swimming toward him. At the same time, he collected Ed Wheaton, who swam by, and the three of them, holding onto the edge of the planking as they swam, reached the raft in safety.

Bud Comet says that Ensign Moore and Chief Wallace then took charge on the raft. They doled out the emergency rations which included a very brief swallow of water each twelve hours. Another raft and net, containing Ensign West and a large group of men, tied up to them. They then drifted together, experiencing the same problems incurred by the other raft group discussed in Chapter 9.

All of the reports and interviews I have heretofore related are recollections fifty years after the fact. Nevertheless, the events were so traumatic, they are indelibly etched in the minds of all the survivors whom I have been able to contact. Fortunately, in my research I uncovered in the files of Robert LeClercq, brother of John LeClercq, a detailed narrative of the events on that 25th of October, off Samar, and the subsequent struggle to survive at sea. Thirteen single-spaced, typewritten pages in length, this account was written by Ens. Jack Moore, the young supply officer from Kansas. Moore, by virtue of the Navy V-12 officer program, had obtained a fine undergraduate education at the University of Pennsylvania, receiving his degree only a few months earlier.

With the facts still vivid in his mind, Moore wrote the initial portion of his account only a few days after rescue, while he and the others were en route from Leyte Gulf to Hollandia on an LST. The concluding portion, dated Wednesday, 22 November 1944, was written on the SS *Lurline*, as he and other survivors neared San Francisco, en route from Hollandia and Brisbane. He sent it, especially, to the parents of John LeClercq so they might better understand, from a firsthand account, what the men of the *Roberts* accomplished and endured. In effect, he told in a short story format, for John's parents, who had little concept of life on a small ship of the navy, who knew nothing about the duties of any of the men who served on board, and who, only faintly, might fathom what might occur in a naval battle — certainly nothing about the rigors of trying to survive at sea. It was an account which they could appreciate. They did, and fortunately, the LeClercq family has preserved it all of these many years. It meant much more to them than the official report from the Navy Department.

It is somewhat dramatic in style, probably as befits a highly educated, perceptive, very young officer who had only thirty days of sea duty at the time of this momentous encounter with the Japanese fleet. Nevertheless, I have never seen a similar account by anyone. His manner of outlining what occurred, his choice of words and subject matter, his characterization of some of those who served and survived with him, proved to be an interesting contrast with the mudane, dry style of the detailed official action reports, concerned only with facts, which I reviewed in Washington.

Recall, also, that Ensign Moore was the most junior officer on the ship. His living quarters, shared with Ensign West, consisted of a tiny, isolated space in the aft area of the ship, just above the churning screws. It was, probably, the least desirable space on the ship. His account begins there, with the usual predawn General Quarters routine. Like supply officers on most ships, his additional duty included encoding and decoding messages; therefore, his GQ station was in the radio shack, adjoining CIC, just below the bridge area of the ship. He entitled his narrative: "A Japanese Admiral's Dream Come True." In order that the parents of a very popular young officer, killed in action, might better understand the spirit of the *Roberts'* officers and crew, and how they performed on that occasion, he began his story.

"Man your battle stations; man your battle stations," came over the loudspeaker in a Southern drawl at five-thirty on the morning of the twenty-fifth of October. I hadn't heard the words in my bunk in the aft officer's quarters for two reasons. One, the speaker wasn't in our compartment and the bulkheads hold out most of the speaker's volume. Second, I had stayed up until four in the morning reading *Young Ames*; consequently, "young Jack" was dead to the world. Mr. West [his roommate] wasn't there to hear and awaken me because he had the four to eight watch. However, he surmised correctly that I wouldn't hear the regular general quarters alarm, since I very seldom had in the past, so, he had the quartermaster on the bridge call me. It was nothing to get particularly excited about since that general quarters was part of our daily routine. We always had them during the breaking of day and every evening at sunset, for it was at these two periods that a ship is most vulnerable to attack. By the time I had dressed, the hatches, which insure water-tight integrity between compartments, had been closed. It had happened before, though, and I had little trouble in making my way forward three compartments and up the ladder and through the water-tight manhole hatch to the main deck. After screwing the hatch back down, I made my way on up to my battle station during GQ, the radio shack.

When I opened the door, the lights went out within the room, but they flashed back on upon closing the door. This was to prevent light leaking out into the semi-darkness of morning. Filing myself behind the row of four chairs, which contained men absorbed in their job of receiving [radio] messages through their earphones, on through the small square room which housed the transmitter units, I took a sharp left and stepped into an even smaller room which contained the electric coding machine. Here, the efforts of the men on the earphones in the other room were broken down on the machine. Meaningless groups, lines, and pages of alphabetical letters were typed into the machine; and in return, the machine spit out a long thin white ribbon bearing coherent words and phrases. My job was to shovel the alphabetical groups into the machine, and then paste the resulting strip on to the message blank in the same manner telegraph messages are pasted on a blank form.

Serafini, chief radioman, was sitting at the machine, evidently having given up hope of my arriving for GQ that morning. When I tossed a sleepy "good morning" at his back, he turned around and returned the greeting. After finishing the line he was typing, he raised his two hundred and twenty pound hulk from the chair and made his way out of the room so I could replace him at the machine. I had gotten to know the chief pretty well during the prior two weeks since heading for the Philippines. For, it was at this time that I had been designated as a decoding officer. He first came to my attention during the Shellback initiation on crossing the equator. He had been the Royal Baby [of King Neptune's], and he played the part perfectly. Imagine if you can a two hundred twenty pound man, who couldn't have been over five feet ten inches in height, stark naked except for a pair of ill-fitting diapers with a big cigar clenched between his teeth. During the ceremony, it was a lowly Pollywogs duty, after having his mouth filled with a Royal Toothpaste of grease, to kiss the navel of the Royal Baby. Between messages at the coding machine, I picked up a great deal of his life in piece-meal lots. He had come over from Italy with his mother when he was nine years old and they had settled in Philadelphia. During the first World War he had served in the Navy while at the age of seventeen. When this current war broke out in forty-one, he enlisted again despite the fact he was a father of two and well over the age limit. But, he figured that the United States had been good to him and those whom he loved, making his years happy ones. Serafini impressed one that he would repay any debt regardless of the personal sacrifice involved. This was his way of repaying our government. I remember making out a check for him one afternoon and later finding it in a letter written to his son. Since it was my duty to censor mail, I read the birthday letter in its entirety. The closing sentences have impressed themselves upon my mind — "Be a good, stout boy and mind your Mommy all the time, even when you think she might be wrong, so that daddy can be proud of his eight year old man when he comes home again. Your loving Daddy. P.S. Keep up the good grades in school." Serafini's entrance into the war was analagous to our country's entrance [onto the world scene]. Both had a difficult go of it when they were young, but they had worked and developed what they had until now it was worth protecting, even if it meant sacrificing their very being.

A goodly number of messages were waiting to be broken down and I immediately regretted leaving my room in such haste, having forgotten to put on my glasses. However, it didn't worry me too much because I intended to pick them up when I went down for breakfast. Five minutes later, the Southern voice drawled over the speaker system, "Cooks and stewards secure from general quarters; cooks and stewards secure from general quarters." Then there was the familiar clang, clang, (a steady tone), clang, clang of the general alarm. Everything was following the regular pattern. At a quarter past six the Southern drawl gave a repeated "All hands secure from general quarters." It was the last time I heard that voice; the voice belonged to the brother of the boy for whom the ship was named, Samuel B. Roberts. Another day had broken. We would be leaving these waters off the coast of Leyte in a couple of weeks.

I was in the middle of a lengthy message, so, I didn't leave the room. At six thirty-two the captain's voice came over the speaker. Everyone dropped their work and listened intently, for, we all knew that it must be important since the captain seldom announced his own words to the crew. He began: "A large Japanese fleet has just been contacted. They are fifteen miles away and headed in our direction. They are believed to have four battleships, eight cruisers, and a number of destroyers. It is our duty to protect the six aircraft carriers in our unit. All right, men, man your battle stations." The click of the switch on the speaker was now quite pronounced in the silence which was now upon us all. Serafini turned to me, cocked his head to one side, pressed his lips so that the lower one was forced out, and then, not expecting a reply from me, turned around and resumed his typing. Wheaton, radio technician 1st class, came over to where I was sitting and said, "What are the odds, Mr. Moore?" I was momentarily taken back by the question, because I realized that here, for the first time, the odds were *not* in our favor. On several previous occasions I had told the fellows to quit worrying and had augmented my instructions with a quoting of estimated odds. When we left Manus and first headed for the invasion, I had quoted to the radiomen odds of ninety to one in favor of our safe return. During the typhoon I had quoted odds of fifty to one in our favor. But, now, I had to quote odds of one to one. Even up. Fifty-fifty chance. Not of our winning the naval engagement, but of our being alive after our naval defeat. For, defeat was obvious. We were six light CVE's, three destroyers and four destroyer escorts. The largest size gun in the whole group was the five inch, while we were to be faced against twelve and fourteen inch shells from the enemy's larger ships. The enemy could move as a unit at thirty knots; we were held back to twenty knots by the aircraft carriers. There was far less armor plate [none] on all of our ships. There was no running away to fight another day when the odds might be in our favor. They were too close and too fast.

While the Jap fleet closed the distance between us at the rate of five miles every half hour, all of the ships were busy laying smoke screens. I ran down to the ship's office and picked up a money list which I had placed in a condom for water-tightness a couple of days before. It could be used for checking the missing and, also, for rebuilding pay accounts in case we were sunk. Mr. Gurnett, the first lieutenant, stopped me in the passageway and told me to pick up a life jacket in the machine shop. I had one, but at this point a second one seemed feasible; especially since I didn't know how good a lifebelt I had. I climbed back to the coding room and sat down at the machine to decode, anything to occupy my mind. The first message was quite short and when I read it I threw it down with disgust. The message emminated from Admiral Nimitz and it read something like this — "Due to the splendid airmanship shown in yesterday's engagements, and with a continuation of such coordinating action, I can assure a defeat of the Japanese Navy from which it will never recover." The message was all right; it just came at the wrong moment. How could the Jap navy have stumbled onto an isolated unit such as ours? Where were our big ships? The questions are unanswerable, so why ask them. I learned partially the answer a few days later in a news item written by John Hughes, C.B.C. correspondent. The Japanese had gathered available naval strength and separated their fleet into two groups. They were to close the pinchers on the United States Leyte Gulf landing . . . [he then describes the Surigao Strait battle in the John Hughes account] . . . [then from the John Hughes account he refers to Kurita's group] moving on Leyte Gulf and coming in the area of our light carrier force, of which the *S.B. Roberts* was a part . . . [as per John Hughes, our group] was there only to provide air coverage for the landing operations at Leyte. Japanese battleships opened fire on the carriers and their escorts. For the Japanese (and I quote this), it was a naval commander's dream come true.

While the big shells from the enemy must have been whistling around us at the time, I was not aware of the fact as I sat impatiently in the decoding room. It was terribly sticky in the little room and I walked out of the radio shack and into the passageway to get a breath of fresh air. The CIC room was adjacent to the radio shack and the door was open. As I looked through the door into the crowded room, my gaze encountered terse expressions upon the faces of all. Mr. Roberts, the executive officer, looked up from the plotting table and met my gaze. Being surprised at his continuing stare, I could think of no more intelligent answer than to wink at him. I don't know his reaction, for he tore his eyes from mine and continued his work on the plotting table. I walked back into the radio shack. Rohde offered me a package of cigarettes from a full carton that I had seen several times propped on his desk. As he handed me the pack, he said with a half-scared grin, "I was saving these to sell for a dollar and a quarter a pack the first time we were ever attacked. I've changed my mine now; they're free."

At seven-twenty-five our five inch guns sounded, shaking me to realize that not only was the enemy in range of our guns, but that we were in range of their guns. The ship was doing some high speed maneuvering because I had to prop my hand against the wall for support. God, what a battle station! Nothing to be seen except the equipment in the room. Silly, meaningless thoughts began tearing through my mind as the din of battle quickly increased. Would the transmitter at my back stop a shell from coming through? In front of me was the coding machine; it only came up to my neck in height. Should I duck? Was I scared? To this overused question there is an overused answer of "I didn't have time to be scared, I was so busy." A shell hit the ship with a "wham"; it wasn't nearly as deafening an explosion as the firing from our own guns. It shook the ship terrifically and there was no doubt about our being hit. I was later informed that the shell hit gun number forty-two, wiping out her crew. Mr. LeClercq was killed by this shell. He was a blonde, amiable lad from Texas and was my age. Whenever anyone asked him for help, he always gave a pleasant "No strain, no strain," for an answer. Several of the crew had picked up that expression from him. I felt I was closer to him than I was to anyone else on the ship. He had been stores officer before I reported aboard. I remember his mother always numbered her letters to him. At Manus he was short ten or eleven letters from her. I glanced at my watch; it was five minutes before eight. Everyone in the radio shack had quit working and was holding on to the desk for support. WHAM! Something big had hit us. The ship writhed in pain for a full half minute before returning to normal position. Bomb? Torpedo? There was no answer to the question, but I didn't ponder over the question very long because, suddenly, the room was filled with hot, thick, suffocating smoke and steam. We jumped up in unison and rushed out of the room en masse. It was coming from the ladder leading down, so, our exit had to be up onto the bridge.

It was my first glimpse of day, and where I had expected to find sunlight, only a heavy mist and remnants of smoke screens were visible at first glance. The air was acrid with gun smoke and it made our eyes smart. Four brilliant yellow blasts could be seen off our starboard bow. I, instinctively, ducked behind a metal railing, although it was quite pointless, for, a twelve inch shell certainly wasn't going to let a thing, a quarter inch slab of metal, halt its flight. She (i.e., enemy ship) was closing in for the kill at an angle. We were dead in the water and our guns had stopped firing except for the forward five inch gun, which was still tossing shells at that cruiser. The captain turned to me, "Pay, tell the engine room to make all available speed. We'll try and duck out of here." My heart sank. Down below was the source of the smoke which had forced us topside. I had been ordered to go down into that inferno. However, some unknown voice said, "Both engines are dead, Captain." "Scuttle the ship then," instructed the captain. I had a flashlight on my belt, so, Mr. Stevenson, the communication officer, and I made our way through the smoke and down into the radio shack. We took the wheels from the coding machine, grabbed secret data from a safe, and climbed back to the bridge to toss them over the side. It took two trips to complete the job.

The bridge was quite crowded with men. The captain gave the order to prepare to abandon ship. I climbed down the ladder behind the bridge onto the torpedo deck. After helping some men break loose one of the life nets, I climbed on down to the main deck. [William] Katsur, my storekeeper striker, was crying. There was a shrapnel wound high on his arm and it was bleeding profusely. The kid is only seventeen. I later heard that he was rescued and had turned out to be quite a man after the captain talked to him on the raft. I bumped into Mr. Moylan, a thin fellow of twenty-two with aspirations of teaching English after all this mess is over, and he turned to me and said with half a grin, "Guess this is really War." I managed a "You said it!" in reply and then helped lay a man on the deck who was wounded in the thigh. Mr. Moylan was picked up (i.e., rescued) and is now aboard a hospital ship; he wasn't wounded, but the long exposure [on a floater net] put him temporarily out of his mind.

Mr. Gurnett, the first lieutenant, called up to the bridge, "I would advise the captain to abandon ship." He was head of the repair parties and his examination of the damage had prompted this advice. I went over to the port side and found my life net in shreds. But, other nets and rafts were now in the water, and besides, my chief concern was to get away from this stationary target. The ship had lost nearly all of her headway. The Jap cruiser had moved in quite close by this time, but for some reason was holding her fire. She couldn't have missed from this range. . . . With the captain's words, "Abandon ship, men. Well done," I stepped over the side, dropped down a couple of feet, and hit the cool Pacific waters. It was around eight-thirty.

Although my kapoc was quite sufficient to keep me afloat, I pressed the lever in my life belt which fired the air cartridges. I could feel it tighten around my waist as I swam strongly away from the ship. After swimming for about five minutes, I turned around to take an inventory of the situation. A magazine was on fire and the exploding shells sounded like firecrackers. I noticed that all of the rafts were drifting off from the starboard stern; and here I was off the port bow by a good hundred yards. I started swimming again, and this time toward the rafts and circumventing the ship. There were three men on the closest raft, which was a good fifty yards away from the ship. Oil covered them from head to foot, making them unrecognizable, as it did me after I hit the fuel oil slick. They didn't recognize me at first and paid no attention to my early calls to wait for me. They shouted back something about getting away from the ship before she went down.

They were really right but I didn't want to take a chance on their drifting away; so I gave out an order, "G — Damnit, you wait for me. We have plenty of time." The chief recognized my battle helmet and my voice this time, so, he had the men stop paddling. It didn't take long to catch up to them, and as I grabbed hold of the raft, I noticed Chief Bos'n mate Wallace and Chief Yeoman Blaszczyk. Others had caught up with the raft, and we now numbered twelve.

I wanted to get the raft away as soon as possible in case the ship decided to take a quick nose dive under. I had heard stories of depth charges going off because they hadn't been put on safety, and I didn't know if the big boy from the Bronx, Emanuel, had had a chance to do it. Exploding depth charges cause severe internal injury. So we all climbed into the water and pulled the raft. After we were a good half mile away, we climbed inside to get a bit of rest.

The Jap cruiser had come in close, fired a couple of shots into the *Roberts* to insure her sinking, and now, was moving off. Another Jap ship had joined her. The men were afraid of their firing at us, but they were quite decent about the way they treated us. They had waited until nearly all of our men had left the ship before coming in for the sinking. I have not seen, nor heard, any authentic proof of the Japs firing upon our life rafts during this engagement. Maybe they were too occupied; but the fact remains that they did not fire upon us.

Around ten o'clock the boilers on the *Roberts* exploded, putting out the fires, but not sinking her. Mr. Gurnett had done a good job in keeping the watertight integrity between compartments. The men wanted to row further away, but I held them up. I wanted to find out if she was going to sink. I had plans of going back to recover food and water if she stayed afloat until afternoon. Maybe she wasn't going to sink after all. She was on an even keel. But, my plans went under with her at eleven o'clock when she abruptly reared her nose perpendicular to the water, paused, and then slipped under without a sound. Emanuel had done a good job of placing the depth charges on safety. No explosions took place as she pulled the blanket of waves over her battered frame. My short, adventuresome, thirty-eight days aboard the good ship, USS *Samuel B. Roberts* (DE-413), were over. Later we learned that this battle had saved the Leyte Gulf [landings]. Turning around and away from where she went under, we now settled down to serious thought of being rescued.

As we were lifted on top of a wave, we could see two groups

of survivors from our ship about a quarter of a mile ahead of us. I said to start pulling after them so that we could tie together. Chief Wallace didn't like the idea of tieing up with such a large group because of the danger of plane attack. He also knew that their raft and life net were overloaded, and that would mean sharing our food and space with more than we had at present. I figured that our chief concern was to be rescued and not with avoidance of enemy attack, so, I let my original orders stand. One of my men had had a hole blown in his life belt, so I gave him one of mine. I had tied an additional flashlight, a whistle, and a pair of sun glasses to it; but, when I cut them off with my sheath knife before giving him the belt, they slipped out of my grasp into the oily waters and went down to the bottom. Most of the men were without head coverage, so I took the metal shell off of my helmet and gave it to another. The man must have lost it during the night, for, I don't recall seeing it the next day.

We caught up with the other group about 1400; they had already tied their raft and life net together. I remember the time because one of the men asked me, and I had to go to a great bit of effort to wipe the oil from the crystal. Nothing was free from the oil and you can't wipe off oil with oil. By pressing down quite hard with my finger, I made a squeegee, which cleared a narrow path on the crystal's surface. We tied on to their life net so that it was riding between the two rafts.

You may know what a Navy life raft and life net are, but before the twenty-fifth of October I confess I had the wrong conception of them. The dimensions of a raft must be about 10' x 8'. From the air they must resemble a square "O." Inside the "O" is a platform held by ropes and submerged about three feet; in other words, [while standing on the platform] you are *always* at least three feet in the water. Strapped to the crossed-lathe bottom are two kegs of water, a can of food, and a container filled with signal apparatus, first aid kit, and cigarettes. As for a life net it has twice as uncomfortable space because there is no ability to stand whatsoever. [Life nets] are composed of hard rubber disks, which resemble hockey pucks, and these are held in groups of eight by rope, which has been interlaced so that it spreads out over the water. It has no rigid framework and there is no protection whatsoever from sharks, a deadly enemy in the Philippine waters.

The two rafts and the net were built to hold forty. We were seventy-eight! Our little raft was almost capsized when the rush of men from the net hit it. There was going to have to be "rationing," with disciplinary backing. Everyone was already at each

other's throat. Everyone's nerves were high strung after the battle.
. . . [with Ensign West, in the other raft, dazed from the battle], I
decided to make our raft headquarters for the three groups [and
took charge]. Chief Wallace was in the raft with me; he had been
sunk twice before this and his experience made him our most valuable occupant. He'll have been in the Navy for twenty years in
1945. Consequently, I made a practice of receiving his advice,
passing judgment on it, and then executing the result.

Our first job was to transfer the seriously wounded from the
net to a raft. A fellow by the name of Thurmond, whom I didn't
know, died before we could transfer him to the raft. He had been
pretty well shot to pieces, and I doubt if he would have lived even
if medical care had been available. That left seventy-seven of us.
There were two others seriously wounded — Osborn, who was
covered with third-degree burns; and Rohde, who had a long, deep
hole in the calf of his leg. Osborn, (a water tender, first class), had
tried to shut off the steam in the engine room. Rohde was the
radioman who had given me the pack of Camels. He informed me
that Chief Serafini, [another radioman], had had an arm blown
off. Here I was with no dependents, unmarried, and scott free of
any injury. When the radiomen received their wounds, I still
haven't been able to find out. I had Osborn moved to the raft, but
I kept Rohde on the net where he could keep his leg free of the
others and where he wouldn't have to put the strain of his weight
on the leg. [Then], a group of American TBF's flew overhead. I
doubt if they saw us.

We all started asking questions as to who had been killed and
wounded. I asked of Joe Green, my second class storekeeper, but
no one seemed to know about Joe. Before the typhoon, a week
earlier, Joe had slipped a note under my papers on my desk —
"Mr. Moore, if something should happen to me in the impending
action, would you please write a note of comfort to my parents.
Thank you, Sir. Joe." Green couldn't swim and had always been
afraid of the water. He was a darn fine storekeeper and a marvel-
ous man with whom to work. As I write this, no further word has
reached me of him. I am praying he was on another raft and has
been picked up. . . . [Suddenly] our hopes were bolstered when
two TBF's came over quite low and dipped their wings. They
would give our position to the ships. Later, I wondered if they
took us for Japs; I know that they couldn't tell by our faces, for,
we were still covered with the thick fuel oil. We talked about the
planes for about an hour, and then I decided to assign men to a raft
or net before it got dark. I placed Ferris, the ship's baker, in charge

of the net. [Note: Ensign West, still somewhat dazed, together with and assisted by Royce Masters, a storekeeper, first class, took charge of the other raft]. There weren't enough positions on the net, so we took twenty-four on (or alongside) our raft. A watch was established aboard each raft and the net to see that men didn't fall asleep and drift away during the darkness.

Night fell fast and early, I think around six-thirty. The waves were quite large and they broke over us all night. We were drifting with our oil slick, which must have covered a good half-mile area, for, we never did escape it despite exerting effort to do so. We had to work shifts in the raft for those who were in fair condition, because only sixteen could crowd into the raft at one time. This meant that eight men had to hang on the outside, (alongside), every half an hour.

There's not much I can write about this night, because of the pitch black darkness. It rained off and on most of the night. Osborn was moaning constantly as I tried to hold his head out of the water. The men were ordered to wrap their arms and legs around each other to take advantage of body warmth. Everyone's teeth were chattering — God, but the water was cold. I saw a can of food break loose once during the night, but it was quickly recovered. The most pronounced memory I have of that night and the following night is the extremely slow passing of time. It seemed like an entire week of darkness. I didn't go to sleep, but several of the men were able to catch an hour or two by having others hold their heads out of the water.

Dawn finally creeped [*sic*] out and everyone felt much better. As soon as there was sufficient light, we took a count and found that all of the men were present and still alive. Remnants of smoke screens were ahead of us. At first, they looked like rows of trees, but this impression didn't last long as we drifted through them. Our sluggish minds were quickened when we heard guns firing off in the distance to our right. After the sun came out we could see a dim outline of land. Chief Wallace estimated it was about fourteen miles away. But, we were drifting away from it. He wanted the men to start pulling for it, but after half an hour, we were losing ground and the men were losing energy — energy that might be used to good advantage in remaining alive. I had the men knock off their efforts. I had no right to assume that we would be picked up before a week's time, and I wanted all of the men to be alive when that day arrived. There was little fear in my mind that we wouldn't be picked up, but I would not let myself hazard a guess as to how long that would be. We knew we were fairly close to shore. . . .

Around eleven o'clock we broke open a five gallon can which contained eighteen cans of concentrated food — malted milk tablets, hard tack, and canned meat. I figured we still had a lot of food in us, so we broke open just a couple of cans of malted milk tablets. This seems quite simple now, but at the time it was quite a feat to dole it out. We cleared the rafts except for the two chiefs and myself. This brought the outside of the raft out of the water and we used it as a workbench. It was difficult to open the canvas covered can because the oil made everything so slick. Finally, we succeeded in pulling out two cans of tablets, but we couldn't make sixteen cans fit back where there had been eighteen; so, we left a couple of cans of hard tack out. Taking my sheath knife, I scraped as much grease from one hand as possible as the men were swimming around to form a line. My efforts were ineffective though, and the two tablets that each man received on his tongue from my fingers were invariably covered with oil.

Men, who didn't know they were wounded the first day out, were now suffering somewhat, and numbered about six. We had to pass them their tablets on the oily lid and then a tablet put between their lips with oily fingers. Oil was beginning to blind several men. The worst part about it was the fact that once you got oil in your eyes you had to wait until it ran out, because there was nothing free of the stuff with which to wipe the eyes clean. I didn't think I would like my tablets, but was pleasantly surprised to find out that they were delicious despite the oil. They must have affected my taste buds for I can still taste them, even now as I write about them. This simple meal was a two hour job and it was afternoon.

We had our hopes aroused again when we saw a TBF and her fighter escort winging their way toward the land we had seen that morning. They were a great distance away, but we broke out our signal mirror in hopes they would return this way. They returned around four o'clock from their bombing mission and passed over and ahead of us. Our signalman had been holding the mirror free of the oily surface for a couple of hours and now he signaled like mad at the two retreating planes. I doubt if they saw us for they continued their course without dipping a wing. This left us all feeling pretty low.

I began to realize what a wide expanse this Pacific covered and how infinitesimally small our group was in comparison to it. I was roused from such dismal thoughts by a cry of "land!" from one of the men. I had mistaken Osborn's groans for airplane motors several times so I raised not too optimistic eyes in the direction [the man's] finger was pointing. It did resemble land, and after several believed they saw land, too, I decided to try pulling for it. After the plane episode of an hour before, I was ready to give up hope of being seen in the water. So, we broke open the two cans of hardtack, along with a couple of more, and handed them to the men. It was difficult to swallow the dry morsel, so we broke out a keg of water and carefully rationed out two ounces per man, with the instructions to swish it around in the mouth before swallowing it. Despite the fact that land was so close, I still wasn't forgetting my schedule of rationing. It was one of the few times in my life that I have been too practical. I planned on making the food and water last for the seventy-seven of us for eight days. We gave out the remainder of a can of malted tablets because water had leaked into the can. Osborn was given four ounces of water. A man had to be assigned to hold his head up all of the time now. The men wanted a cigarette, but I figured it wouldn't do them any good, so, I refused their requests.

It was twilight when we started out for the land in the distance. The chief marked a star ahead of us and a star behind us so that we could set some sort of a course when it became dark. As darkness closed in, we saw a green light off to our right in an opening in a smoke screen. A Jap Sally came gunning out of the same screen and flew over us quite low. At first we thought it had taken off from a carrier, but then we realized that a twin-engine bomber of her size must be land based. She's really a trim craft and deserving of her name, "Slick Sally." I realized then that we were going into Jap held land, and I didn't know if I had the right to take seventy-six men in to become prisoners of the enemy. So, we held a vote as to what action we should follow. First, I explained to the men about the wounded men; they needed medical attention badly. Some of the stronger men wanted to take a raft in to the shore and take their chances on evading the enemy, but I gave them a flat "No" for an answer. We had come this far as a unit and we were going to stay this way; whatever we did would be done as one group. After this, nearly all of them were in favor of pulling ashore, and, if possible, to hide away in the hills.

It wasn't as dark as the night before, but still the moon was hiding behind the clouds most of the time. We swam, (pulling and pushing the raft unit), for what seemed days before we finally saw another green light to the right of us. It would blink on for half a minute every five minutes. As we started pulling toward it, another light was seen to our rear. It was an orange light, which blinked in the same pattern as the green. The tide was carrying us in, now; for, most of the men were exhausted and had stopped swimming, yet, we were moving towards shore. We lost the lights when we drifted into a smoke screen. I told all of the men to stop and rest, since there was no objective in view. I decided to stay awake and watch.

Rohde was out of his head, as was Harrington and several others. Men were begging me to allow them to get in the raft. They felt they were too weak to hold onto the outside, or to re-main on the net. I was amazed at the number who were ready to give up and who wanted to die. Several felt they were weaker than others on the raft, and they might have been right, but who was I to tell which man was the weaker in a group of weak men. When some of the men had grumbled when I refused them cigarettes earlier in the afternoon, I had shouted to them, "You men are go-ing to hate me before we'er picked up, but, by God, there are go-ing to be seventy-seven live men when that time comes."

No one had commented on my words, and I felt that already they were mad at me. And now, Rohde was asking me if it was all right to go below for a little rest before he went on watch! Har-rington was himself most of the time, but occasionally he would burst out with some non-sensical orders, or such things as: "Here, Captain, let me take the wheel for awhile. I'll get us back on course." He was a first class bos'n, and a darned good one, too. I had heard Mr. Gurnett praise his work many a time as a handler of men. A great big, husky, red-headed man of twenty-one, he had been one of the best men of the group, and now, he was becoming delirious. If this happened to him, what about the weaker shadows on the net? Seventy-seven men, seventy-seven men, all live men, when we'er picked up, I had promised seventy-seven live men. I had to get hold of myself.

Every once in a while a body would float away and someone would go retrieve it. How many would be alive in the morning? With these thoughts running through my mind, I must have dozed off, for the next thing I remember the chief was shaking me. We were still in the midst of smoke screens, but the water had become quite smooth. I was really jolted to full wakefulness when I heard a "clink" in the shadows ahead of us. Metal upon metal was the only combination that caused that kind of a sound. Like the closing of a breech of a large gun! We tried to rouse the men in order to start pulling ashore, but to no avail. Everyone had given their all earlier, and now they were so weak that nothing could get them to work. We were drifting away from the noise. I was mad and disappointed. We had been within fifty yards of land and couldn't muster enough strength among us to make the distance to land.

We drifted through one smoke screen after another, each of them looked like trees on land. We saw an orange light to the left of us. A patrol boat was half a mile away and it was using a searchlight. Maybe they had heard my shouts to the men to pull these last fifty yards. Their light was playing over our heads and never did come close to us. I gathered all available flashlights. If they were Japs, and I later learned that they were, we could reasonably hope for hospitalization for our wounded. It was a futile attempt, though; all of the lenses were covered with black fuel oil. Those of us who were still awake became silent. We decided to wait for morning.

The next morning was clear and we could see that we had drifted out almost half way to our original starting position of the previous afternoon. The tide was still carrying us out from the land, so we climbed out of the rafts and started pulling against the current. When we rested, I took a count of the men and was very pleased to find that we had lost no men during the night. Rohde was still in a bad way, and Osborn had lapsed into unconsciousness.

We were about ready to continue our losing battle with the tide, when Chief Blaszczyk saw the masts of several ships to our left. I was convinced they were enemy craft even then, and besides, they didn't appear to be coming towards us. So, we started pulling against the tide again in order to be close to shore when it changed again in our favor. On our next rest, I began to take an interest in the ships. They had veered toward us and although they were still too far away to see us, they began to encircle us. As they came within a mile of us, I could make out their superstructures. They were different from any I had ever seen. They sloped to the rear like an airflow Chrysler. There was no doubt in my mind now as they moved within a half a mile of us. I turned to the survivors, "Men, it looks as if we'er going to be picked up by the Japs. We'er covered with fuel oil and they won't be able to tell we'er Americans until they get right upon us. They may fire upon us. If they do, act as if you have been hit, quickly."

"But, Mr. Moore, those are LCI's," said Harrington at my side. It made me mad because I felt he was giving false optimism to the others. After all, his eyes looked like fish eyes they were so pale from the searing fuel oil. And, hadn't he been hysterical the night before! I hadn't changed my opinion at all. I became hopeful when a ship came steaming straight at us from our right, because it looked like an American PC. I still wasn't convinced that I was wrong. The flag looked too narrow for it to be a United States ship. Other eyes much better than mine saw what I could not, and their owners had started shouting and slapping each other on the back before I realized that we were saved.

It's hard to describe that feeling I felt inside of me as the PC pulled in close enough to recognize us for Americans. They lowered their guns and commenced to make ready to take us aboard. Masters started to swim for the ship, but I called him back; we weren't going to get a man caught in the ship's screws. The first thought that ran through my mind was that seventy-seven men were alive as I had promised, even though it was through no efforts of mine that they were here. What if we had made the shore the night before! My second thought was the money list in the prophylactic. I felt in my pocket. Yes, it was still there.

My hilarious happiness was short lived. Someone on the other raft called over: "Mr. Moore, I believe Osborn is dead." I jumped out of the raft and swam over to the one containing Osborn. I grabbed his arm and tried to find his pulse. I thought I detected a slight murmur. Forgetting my orders to Masters, I swam toward the PC until I was within calling distance. "Throw me a line so you can take aboard a man who is either dead or just about so, first." I caught the second line and swam back to the raft with it. Grabbing Osborn with my free hand, I had them pull us in. I lost my helmet as we were being towed toward the ship. We were hauled aboard, Osborn in a stretcher and me up the ladder on the side of the ship. I faintly remember banging my chin on the ladder, but I didn't mind. A cup of coffee was waiting for me and I declined a cigarette. A man helped me take off my oily clothes. When emptying my pockets, I discovered that I had lost the money list. To lose it five minutes before being picked up is definitely a Jack Moore stunt!

By this time all of the men were aboard and climbing out of their clothes at the same time they gulped down hot coffee. They had some diesel oil to take the worst of the fuel oil [off of our bodies], and then we were led down to the most delicious pancakes I ever expect to eat. The skipper of the PC knew Commander Copeland, our Captain. [After I ate]; he took me down to his stateroom and gave me some clean clothes to put on. I tried to shave but cried all the while because I had my chin covered with sores from rubbing against my kapoc in the mixture of fuel oil and salt water. As I write this, I still haven't shaved a second time, but the sores are healing rapidly. As I prepared to go below to get some much needed rest, one of our men informed me that Osborn had died five minutes after being brought aboard. The burns and exposure had been too much for him. I had the Captain of the PC count my money, but I never did get a chance to receive a written verification from him.

Some other men from one of the aircraft carriers had been picked up earlier. I learned that our captain, the executive officer, the first lieutenant, the communications officer, a gunnery officer, and Mr. Moylan had been picked up earlier, but were on one of the LCI's. I still don't know how many enlisted men they had with them. I, also, learned that we had probably lost two aircraft carriers, two destroyers, and our ship in the battle. How the others got away I'll probably never know. It seems our loss was quite worthwhile.

Through our delaying action the American forces were given sufficient time to prepare for the enemy's attack on Leyte Gulf. Consequently, the enemy had received a terrific beating; one from which Admiral Nimitz says they will never recover.

I slept until twelve that night, and the following morning around five o'clock we were transferred to a large operations ship. Here we were issued some new clothing, given food and rest, and a chance to collect our senses. Rohde and a couple of others were transferred to a hospital ship. I saw Mr. Stevenson and learned what information I have given about the occupants of the other group of survivors. In the afternoon, I filled out clothing chits so that my men could get clothing issued to them. My name was called about four p.m., along with Mr. West's, but he had gone back to the PC to see about getting Osborn buried. I had been given his [Osborn's] high school graduation ring and his wedding band by the PC's doctor. The band reads on the inside rim — Anita to Jeff 5-7-44. I heeded the loudspeaker call and soon found myself headed for the LST on which I am at present. We're headed for Hollandia and should reach there in the morning. After Hollandia, we're all hoping for the States. There are only twelve enlisted men aboard with me. Mr. Roberts is on the LST in front of us, and the others are on LST's in this group.

It's really nice to loaf around and stay in bed 'til noon. I eat like a horse. I'm fast forgetting that I'm a survivor.

* * * * * * * * *

Wednesday, 22 Nov. 1944

It's been almost a month since our ship was sunk and from the time we were picked up to the present is another story. We reached Hollandia around the fourth of November and sat around waiting for the angels of mercy to take care of us. The angels of mercy must have been on leave, for, after two days of waiting, we were still on the LST with no prospects for a future change. I contacted Mr. Roberts, our executive officer, and we went over to the USS *Wright*, a flagship for the Seventh Fleet. Mr. Roberts did a great deal of work getting us orders. Work, which we later discovered, was wasted. Meanwhile, I was racing around getting my claim approved for my possessions which went down with the ship. I became acquainted with Lt. (jg) Fallon, the disbursing officer aboard the *Wright*, and he assisted me in getting myself some clothes.

Two days were spent ashore, getting clothes for the survivors from the Navy and the Army. One night, three of us had to remain ashore because it was too late to get back to the ship, which was anchored on the opposite side of the harbor. A supply corps commander fixed us with a place to sleep. Living conditions are really rugged on Hollandia. Typical of all tropical islands, the atmosphere is hot and humid. Malaria, Chinese rot, athletes' foot and other fungus diseases are present; but, the disease which exacts the heaviest toll and with the worst effect is dengue, a combination of jaundice and malaria. All of those stationed on the island have turned a greenish yellow from continual use of adabran [sic] tablets to ward off malaria. Fresh water is quite scarce and all must stand in line for a bucket of the precious liquid. Only the mess halls make any pretense of screening-in. The most luxurious bed is the lowly cot equipped with a mesquito netting. The pendulum of moisture swings swiftly from an extreme degree of wetness to an extreme degree of dryness. It is either mud up to your knees or dust over your head. The place is overcrowded and short on supplies. No fresh food is served and none is available for war weary ships going back into the Philippine area. Here in all this muck and squalor, and, living under identical conditions is a large detachment of WACS, Army nurses, and Red Cross workers . . . [in] Hollandia Hell.

The night of the eighth a LCVP carried us from the LST to the shore, where we were quartered for the night. The next morning we packed into trucks which carted us to the floating hotel in which we are at present, the *SS Lurline*. She's a mammoth Matson luxury liner, now chartered by the Army and Navy. She brought a load of WACS and replacement personnel to Hollandia, where some two thousand survivors took their place aboard her. The enlisted men's orders read thirty days leave in the States, while mine instruct me to the Twelfth Naval District in San Francisco for further orders. I'm hoping for thirty days leave, naturally.

[At Hollandia] we were still at the dock on the tenth, and most of the *Roberts'* officers were still without [a change of] clothing. I was the supply officer and the only one with money, so, I hitch-hiked eight miles back into the jungle and hills to an army base which had a supply of khaki. Sizes were limited, and large, so I ended up making three-fourths of my purchases from the WACS' store.

We pulled out the next morning and later on in the day were told that we were headed for Brisbane, Australia. Everything has been most enjoyable from that day to the present. We play volley ball every day on the tennis deck, and evenings find us in a game of bridge or attending a movie in one of the two large dining rooms. It's difficult to describe the immensity of the vessel. She has a laundry, barber shop, tailor, dentist, hospital, two large dining halls, elevators running throughout the ship, bathtubs in every room, chairs on the open deck for sun bathing, volley ball court, tile floors, and every other facility which is to be found in large American hotels. We even have a number of women aboard and a dance is usually held on the tennis deck after the sun goes down. The food is the most delicious I have eaten since rationing went into effect back in the States. Ice cream and cake every evening, fresh salads and vegetables every meal, fresh bacon and eggs every morning for breakfast, all served by stewards who have been aboard since pre-Pearl Harbor days. Oh, it's a great life alright!

I was kept quite busy while en route to Brisbane in giving out clothing, toilet articles, and at the same time reconstructing pay accounts for the 130 men from the *Roberts* who are aboard. Masters, my only storekeeper aboard, and four recruited yeomen worked in shifts with me, and we beat the docking hour by half a day. No one was allowed ashore except those with business important enough to wrangle a pass from the ship's office. Pay of the crew was enough to get me ashore. After leaving the cards at a naval disbursing office and setting up a pattern for their storekeepers, I went shopping in Brisbane. The city is much like any American city except that it's about ten years behind us. The clothes are very plain and cut in the pattern of America's early thirties. Australia's people are quite amiable, but with a hand on the pocketbook. I had dinner with a friend of Jim Fallon, the disbursing officer on the *Wright*, and thoroughly enjoyed four glasses of fresh milk, my first since leaving the States.

I held pay day the following morning and then went ashore

for more sightseeing and shopping. At five o'clock the pubs, or bars, open. Three of us made our way to the Red Cross Center, a square block of buildings provided for entertainment of Americans in Brisbane. We attended the officers' club and became tipsy on four glasses of high-percentage Aussie beer. After dinner we went skating. And, after bruising ourselves properly, we shoved off to the city hall where a dance was in progress. We had a lot of fun dancing the hokey-pokey, which must be a foreign cousin to the Virginia Reel, the Big Apple and the Louis-Braddock fight. When my ninety-two pound partner jumped into a jitterbug on a fast number, even her blarney speech couldn't bring back the foreign atmosphere; so, we shoved off to a tram stop where we caught an open air job like they have in San Francisco. I felt like a survivor by the time I hit the sack.

The next day we shoved off and are now headed for San Francisco with an arrival date set at the 2nd of December.

Serafini died from the loss of blood in the water. Green, my storekeeper, is optimistically listed as "missing." Katsur, storekeeper striker, is not aboard, but they tell me his wounds are not serious. The captain threw his leg out of joint when he fell trying to climb up into a top bunk the morning he was picked up. He is hobbling around on crutches. Mr. Moylan has recovered remarkably fast and his chief difficulty at the present is with his hearing. Mr. Riebenbauer and Mr. Trowbridge, the ship's engineering officers, are given up for dead. Losses are not as great as previously estimated, but still quite severe — 125 enlisted men and 8 officers are alive and accounted for, leaving 93 either dead or missing. Survivors from the two carriers and two destroyers that were sunk in the same action are aboard.

Word came over the radio a couple of nights ago that the Navy has announced the loss and names of the ships. I'm praying that my letter I wrote in Hollandia, has reached home. I couldn't find an airmail stamp on the base, so it may be a month in reaching my family.

Thus, this most illuminating recapitulation account of events, most of which was written only four or five days following the rescue, abruptly ends. Delivered by the author to the parents of John LeClercq, it has been deeply treasured by that family. It made them very proud of the character of the men with whom their eldest son served and with many of whom he had died in battle. It certainly meant more to them than the terse, routine, formal note of condolence from the Navy Department.

Arriving at San Francisco on 4 December, the *Lurline* and its cargo of survivors were greeted as heroes by the citizens of that city. As Mel Harden wrote me:

> Arriving off San Francisco, we were met by a number of small boats bearing "welcome home" signs. Some boats were carrying newspaper people. Those boats escorted our ship into the bay and under the Golden Gate Bridge. . . . At the pier they had a large band and a large crowd of people to greet us. They, also, had a special edition of the newspaper welcoming the survivors, but most of the stories were about a local hero, the commanding officer of the *Gambier Bay*. We all crowded to the port side to see what was going on. This caused the ship to list so badly that they had to make everyone return to their berthing areas before the ship could be docked.

Dudley Moylan vividly recalled the great roar, the tremendous outpouring of sheer joy, that went up from the survivors as they passed under the Golden Gate Bridge. It was a moment he would never forget. Tom Stevenson remarked that they were given money for appropriate blue wool uniforms and taken to Treasure Island to be outfitted. Since the uniforms would not be available for a few days, he and the other officers went "on the town" that evening in their old piecemeal, makeshift khakis that had been scrounged up along the way. This quickly drew the attention of shore patrol units, but their explanation was accepted and they all enjoyed a great evening in San Francisco.

In a few days everyone received thirty days of leave, following which they would be given their new assignments. After the ordeal which they had endured, every survivor eagerly looked forward to a brief, peaceful time at home with loved ones whom they had not seen for so long.

11

Finale

If one reads the newspaper articles published during the end of October 1944, no mention will be found of the heroic action of the men on the three destroyers and four destroyer escorts in Taffy 3. The paucity of information thereon is appalling, but understandable.

That Admiral Halsey left San Bernardino unguarded by taking Task Force 34 with him as he steamed north with all of Task Force 38; that Admiral Kinkaid and Admiral Nimitz were misled by the poorly worded message of Halsey regarding the groups he was taking north with him; that Halsey fell for the Japanese "bait"; that warnings about Kurita's apparent movements had not been heeded by Halsey nor his staff during the night — all of this was too embarrassing, especially to Halsey. He had assumed that Kinkaid would guard San Bernardino Strait, although only Halsey's ships had done this since the invasion of Leyte had begun on the 20th. Furthermore, Halsey knew that Kinkaid's major ships were engaged in the battle raging during the night at Surigao Strait. Apparently, Halsey must have felt that Taffy 1, 2, and 3 were capable of guarding San Bernardino Strait, and could give a warning that would enable Kinkaid's large ships to rapidly move into position. But that would not be possible since Kinkaid's major fleet elements were far to the south at Surigao Strait, still mopping up from its battle which ended just prior to dawn on the 25th.

If there had been a unified command for the Leyte operations, rather than the divided command which existed, then such a lack of coordination could not have occurred. But, by virture of this horrible snafu, it fell to the lot of the men of Taffy 3, alone, to face up to Kurita's overwhelming force that morning, off Samar.

I was most fortunate to confer at length with Mr. H. S. (Gus) Edwards, of Abilene, Texas, regarding many matters concerning the Leyte operations — especially the situation on the *Wasatch* that fateful 25th of October. Mr. Edwards, a former lieutenant USNR, was the cartographic and photographic officer on that ship during various invasions, including Leyte. He vividly recalled the tense situation which occurred on the *Wasatch* when Admiral Kinkaid finally became aware that Admiral Halsey did not have Task Force 34 nearby. Kinkaid clearly understood that Kurita, with his overwhelming firepower, would move into Leyte Gulf and wipe out the American units which were present.

As has been noted, the *Wasatch* was the flagship upon which Kinkaid was embarked; the *Nashville* was the flagship upon which MacArthur was embarked. These two flagships, each with two of these four destroyers for antisubmarine patrol — the USS *Ammen*, USS *Mullany*, USS *Abner*, and the USS *Bush* — were in the transport anchorage of San Pedro Bay, about six miles from the town of Tacloban. Two other destroyers, the USS *McNair* and the USS *Mertz*, were furnishing antisubmarine patrol for transports and supply ships which were at anchor that morning. These were the only naval ships that could immediately engage Kurita if he steamed onward some fifty more miles into San Pedro Bay of Leyte Gulf.

Mr. Edwards advised me that the custom had been for the *Wasatch* and the *Nashville* to remain at anchor during the day, but for security, they put to sea in the area near Taffy 2 each night with their screening destroyers. Fortunately, they had not done this the night of the 24th, and thus were nowhere near Kurita when Kurita made his entrance upon the scene the morning of the 25th.

When Kinkaid learned of the absence of Halsey's Task Force 34 and that a perilous situation was developing, MacArthur was whisked ashore to a house near Tacloban in the PT boat used by the two flagships. As the morning progressed, Mr. Edwards walked out onto the boat deck, and, having been an engineering officer earlier on the *Dorothy L. Dix* (AP-67), he noticed the *Wasatch* was now riding very high in the water. He inquired of a passing engineering officer as to why this most unusual condition existed. He was told that Kinkaid had ordered the ballast to be pumped out in order to produce a shallow draft. If Kurita arrived, and if the *Nashville*, those six screening destroyers and the *Wasatch* were overwhelmed, then the *Wasatch* could make an attempt to escape through the extremely narrow and very shallow San Juanico Strait, which lies between Leyte and Samar Islands. If successful, they could then proceed into the Sibuyan Sea. However, if the *Wasatch* became grounded in San Juanico Strait, then the ship was to be abandoned and everyone would take to the nearby hills. Such an escape would be a desperate last move.

Fortunately, because of the outstanding bravery and daring of the men of Taffy 3, our forces at Leyte were saved. But, as stated at the outset of this chapter, the American public was not told of this bravery, this daring, and this sacrifice, especially as performed by the men on those three destroyers and four destroyer escorts. To have reported this action would have necessitated a complete explanation of the cause of this encounter. Thus, the action off Samar must have been heavily censored, for newspaper accounts in the days immediately following such battle do not mention the destroyers and destroyer escorts involved; not even the names of the *Johnston*, the *Hoel*, or the *Roberts* which so valiantly fought, gave their all, and were sunk.

The usual detailed accounts of military actions covered in the *New York Times* clearly demonstrate this lack of information regarding what really happened off Samar. There are significant articles, with large headlines, telling of our great success in the battle at Surigao Strait; the initial pounding of Kurita on the 24th by Halsey's carrier planes (a pounding which we now know to be somewhat exaggerated) when Kurita made his first attempt to enter San Bernardino Strait; and the sinking of the *Princeton*. The reports regarding Kurita's first attempt boasted that he had suffered so many casualties that he turned back and was fleeing to the west. As to the sinking of the *Princeton*, the press releases indicate that it was the result of a heavy air attack by the enemy. We now know that a lone Japanese plane managed to drop one 500-pound bomb through a break in the overcast, and that the bomb exploded in a critical area of the *Princeton*.

Even when referring to Samar, it is the Jeep carriers that are mentioned. Among the matters summarized by the *Times* on 26 October is only a slight reference to the action off Samar as follows:

> The enemy's northern force [i.e., Kurita], four battleships, several cruisers with destroyers, gained contact with one of our escort carrier groups, [i.e., Taffy 3], off the east coast of Samar and attacked by gunfire. Our *planes* [my emphasis] from that group, supported by those of another group, drove off the attacking fleet, forcing it to retire. . . . Ship casualties sustained by our forces were one escort carrier sunk and several escort carriers and destroyers *damaged* [my emphasis].

Even the summary, which appeared in the Hanson W. Baldwin column of the *New York Times* later that week, does not mention the gallant fight by the men on the three destroyers and four destroyer escorts which were part of Taffy 3. Not because he knew and chose to ignore it, for the battle fought off Samar by this intrepid little force would have been a major public interest story, but undoubtedly because naval censorship dictated subject matter which would be released to the press corps.

Baldwin's summary referred to the great battle at Surigao Strait, the destruction of Ozawa's force of carriers (never referred to as the "bait"), the action off Samar when carrier planes repulsed the enemy, and the previous loss of the *Princeton*.

Again, he mentioned the loss of an escort carrier and damage to several ships. Kept in the dark by censorship, Baldwin stated: "The Japanese pattern of strategy in these desperate attacks is not yet clear." Yet, after Samar, to Halsey and the other commanders it was very clear what had been intended. Since the men of Taffy 3 saved the day, the navy must have felt that it was better, in the press releases, to omit the details as to how and why Samar occurred.

In news articles dealing with our casualties in the Second Battle of the Philippine Sea (as the press called this four-day engagement), the tally of our ships lost and damaged are lumped together initially by types — not by name. By the way the first press releases were worded, one who was not knowledgeable concerning the Battle of Leyte Gulf might be inclined to think that the *Johnston*, the *Hoel*, and the *Roberts* had been in the portion of such battle which took place at Surigao Strait, rather than the portion which occurred at Samar.

This oversight to the public was disclosed by articles published months later, and by subsequent books written after the war. Three very interesting magazine articles appeared in 1945. Two were published in the *American Magazine* of April 1945, one by Rear Adm. C.A.F. Sprague USN, the commander of Taffy 3, entitled "The Japs Had Us On The Ropes"; the other by Capt. Amos T. Hathaway USN, the skipper of the *Heermann*, entitled "The Battle As I Saw It." The third article was by Lt. Robert C. Hagen USNR, senior surviving officer of the *Johnston*, entitled "We Asked For the Jap Fleet — and Got It." This was published in the May 26 issue of the *Saturday Evening Post*. The most recent, and a very authoritative book on this subject, is entitled: *The Battle of Leyte Gulf*, by Thomas J. Cutler (HarperCollins, NY 1994). Mr. Cutler is a retired lieutenant commander, United States Navy, former professor at the Naval War College, and lecturer at the Naval Academy. His book is an exhaustive analysis of this great naval battle which occurred over a four-day period, and his extensive treatment of the actions of the three destroyers and four destroyer escorts in Taffy 3 rectifies the press oversight of late October 1944.

Why did Kurita turn back and depart when it appeared he had victory in sight? This has been debated by naval historians. It was a subject of major proportions at the Admiral Nimitz Symposium in October 1994, which I attended in Kerrville, Texas. In fact, subjects discussed at that symposium piqued my interest; they stirred me to write this book. Once I was apprised of the facts regarding the action off Samar and the gallantry of the men on a little ship like the *Roberts*, I could not wait to locate survivors, review official records, and relate the history of that ship.

Among the items uncovered in my research were the interrogations of Admiral Kurita and other officers, which were conducted in Tokyo after the war. Kurita's occurred on 16–17 October 1945. He admits that he thought he was attacking cruisers and some of Halsey's major carriers. He further stated that this mistaken identity was caused partly by the poor visibility resulting from the smoke which, tactically, was used extremely well by the United States ships. While he wanted to keep his fleet together, the torpedo attacks caused his formation to scatter, and he ordered each ship to fight on its own. He also thought that he had seen masts of other carriers to the east. He had listened to our voice radio transmissions, which had stated it would take roughly two hours to bring aid to Taffy 3. So he knew that he had only a short time to fight before other aid would arrive, and that this aid would be from carrier aircraft. He had no report that Ozawa had been successful in luring Halsey away from the area, so he feared that he would encounter air attacks by planes from the large carriers which had attacked him the day before.

During this engagement with Taffy 3, Kurita received a message that Nishimura, of the Southern Force, had failed. Kurita had not received air support from any land-based planes, he had no messages from Tokyo, and he made a "momentary decision" to turn north. He said that he signaled the order to turn away after a significant air attack, although it did little damage to his ships. At first he thought he would try to aid Ozawa, but, suffering air attacks and getting low on fuel, he went back through San Bernardino Strait, leaving the scene of battle.

At that symposium in Kerrville, one speaker suggested that perhaps Kurita was totally exhausted. Remember, his initial flagship was sunk by our submarines and he was fished from the water while moving through the Palawan Passage. Then, for three days he had had little, if any, rest or sleep. Perhaps he just thought it best to save his ships and retreat; that the Japanese *Sho-Go* plan had failed and that his group might be the only survivor of the three forces.

When the Americans read Kurita's signal hoist to disengage and turn away, they were in utter disbelief, but overjoyed. On the *Fanshaw Bay*, a signalman on the signal bridge, in an act of exceptional bravado, was heard to exclaim: "Oh hell. They're getting away!"

If Kurita had continued to press the battle just a little longer, he would have had the benefit of the kamikaze attacks which began in earnest later that morning. The very first kamikaze attack of the war was upon the *St. Lo*. The log book of the *Raymond* indicates it occurred at 1050, while the log book of the *Fanshaw Bay* says 1052. This attack was successful, and a photograph of the exploding carrier appears elsewhere in this book.

Mr. Fred P. Nickless, Jr., of Manchester, Massachusetts, who was the quartermaster of the watch, stationed on the bridge of the *St. Lo* when that attack occurred, witnessed the attack, and gave me a detailed account thereof as follows:

> Some things happen in one's life that are indelibly impressed on one's mind. I well remember that kamikaze. I was quartermaster of the watch, and our skipper, Captain Francis J. McKenna,

was on the bridge along with the Officer of the Deck. Captain McKenna first spotted the Jap planes — four of them. The look-outs simply missed them. Captain Mac said — "Those are Jap planes, sound the general alarm." I looked where the captain was pointing, and saw them flying very low, only a few feet over the water, coming in aft of the last ship in our formation, on a course parallel to our own. As I watched, they suddenly rose in the air, banked to starboard and flew in aft of us. . . .

While standing on the starboard side of our bridge I could clearly see the four planes until they were directly aft of our ship. Rushing to the port side of the bridge, I was able to see one of the planes coming directly at us; it dropped down so fast I thought it appeared to be ready to strafe us. I could see the bursts of rounds from our 20MM and 40MM guns heading at that plane. If any of them struck the plane, they in no way changed the attack.

Then that plane plunged onto our flight deck. Immediately, I recognized the danger of flying debris, and ducked back into the shelter of the island structure of our ship. Not Captain Mac! He just stood and watched the whole thing. Those of us on the bridge were lucky to escape injury when pieces of that plane and of our flight deck came down on the bridge. One very hot and smoky piece of the plane landed right at my feet. I don't think anyone on the bridge was hurt by this first explosion, but I don't know what happened afterwards as I was too busy trying to make entries in the ship's log.

In only a few minutes the captain gave the order to abandon ship [after other violent explosions occurred]. I went down a line on the starboard side of the bridge, stopped off on the catwalk at the flag bag level, and began to assist others. But one incredible explosion wiped out any confidence I had left, and I just dropped into the water. Looking around, I watched our ship sink. Shortly thereafter I was rescued when the DE's moved in to pick up survivors.

In the event this new and terrifying weapon, the kamikaze, had been combined and coordinated with Kurita's massive firepower, the outcome in Leyte Gulf might have been quite different.

Therefore, if Taffy 3 had not been successful in deterring Kurita, there is no way to guess what the results and ramifications may have been. Wiping out Taffy 3 and proceeding into San Pedro Bay, Kurita's vastly superior force could have played havoc with our forces ashore. At this point, our forces had one leg ashore and one leg still in the water, so to speak. Our supplies, gathered over months for this invasion, could have been destroyed. In the face of heavy enemy naval firepower from the sea, coordinated with Japanese army units attacking from land, our amphibious troops could have been overwhelmed. Would MacArthur have had to flee again? What a press story that would have been! And, if Kurita had then moved on down Leyte Gulf to exit through Surigao Strait, he would have encountered Oldendorf's ships — now short on armor-piercing ammunition from the engagement which had occurred only hours before. Kurita's vastly superior firepower not only could have caused more havoc, but may have allowed his escape. Halsey and his Task Force 38 would have been too far away to render any assistance.

Thus, if Kurita had been a Halsey, if Kurita had been known as "Bull" Kurita, one can imagine many different consequences.

How would the American people have reacted to a military tragedy which could have been comparable to Dunkirk or to the attack on Pearl Harbor? What effect upon the hotly contested presidential election only days away? President Roosevelt was in the political battle of his life for a fourth term, and Governor Dewey was making a serious challenge. Faced with a terrible defeat at Leyte, and a resulting change of administrations, might we have accepted something less than unconditional surrender by the Japanese?

In this respect, also remember that Russia had never declared war on Japan, despite our urging. These two countries were at peace with each other, with full embassy staffs in their respective capitals. Once Germany was defeated and our European troops moved to the Pacific Theatre, would Japan and Russia begin to cooperate? The recently declassified Japanese diplomatic communications, known as the "Magic" intercepts, reveal that the Japanese had considered making an attempt to join with Russia to carve up Asia, much as Hitler and Stalin had done to Poland. With the United States facing Russian strength in Europe, and with no assistance from Russia against Japan, could Russia have played a part in getting us to settle with Japan so it and Japan could divide Asia? If, under such a hypothetical scenario, a deal between Russia and Japan had materialized, would we have had to use "the bomb" elsewhere than in Japan?

One can build various possible, even probable, scenarios. The successful world order that, in fact, came about by our conclusion of World War II could have been quite different.

Therefore, the occurrence off Samar the morning of 25 October

1944 is highly important. Taffy 3 not only saved Halsey's reputation, it saved the invasion of Leyte and it certainly shortened the war.

While initially the public may have been kept in the dark regarding the details of the action off Samar and of what the men of Taffy 3 accomplished, they were well known to the various commanders in the Seventh Fleet. Their various action reports, which I have reviewed in the Operation Archives at the Washington Navy Yard, detail what occurred that day and why they occurred. These reports were top-secret, only declassified long after the war ended. They give due credit, credit which was not publicized in the October press releases. As Admiral Sprague, commander of Taffy 3, commented in his Special Action Report of 29 October 1944: "The high degree of skill, the unflinching courage, the inspired determination to go down fighting, of the officers and men of my command cannot be too highly praised."

As a result of similar comments, Taffy 3, officially known as Task Unit 77.4.3, received the Presidential Unit Citation, a copy of which appears in Appendix C.

Based upon the data which I have reviewed, the men of Taffy 3 deserve the undying admiration of Americans for their courage, their spunk, their fortitude and their devotion to duty which they so amply displayed at Samar.

The 25th day of October 1944 is, indeed, a proud day for America in the annals of its military lore.

12

Requiem

Before the story of the *Roberts* is over, it is appropriate to remember that many men from it and the *Johnston* and the *Hoel* died
at sea due to the utter lack of prompt rescue efforts. Wounds un-
treated, long exposure to the elements, and the presence of sharks
all took a heavy toll. Such loss of life clearly would have been re-
duced by quick and effective rescue efforts. With so many American
ships in the area operating in known waters, in retrospect it seems as
though more rapid rescue efforts could have been effected. The navy
had detailed procedures for downed airmen from carriers — as airmen were highly skilled and very valuable personnel that could not
be easily replaced. Recall how quickly Lt. (jg) George Bush was rescued from the sea when his plane was ditched. The navy knew where
each ship was operating at all times, and in the Bush case, a submarine in the area was ordered to temporarily cease its patrol and make
an immediate rescue. Apparently, there was no such detailed procedure in effect for men of surface ships lost in battle.

The long delay in effecting a rescue, when there were so many
ships of various types available in the area, was commented upon by

men from the various ships in their interrogations which took place on the *Lurline* and elsewhere.

A narrative by Lt. Maurice F. Green USNR, a survivor from the *Hoel*, comments on the number lost at sea due to the delayed rescue efforts. He said that it was well known that the commanding officer of the USS *Hazelwood*, a destroyer in their own squadron and a part of Taffy 1 which had raced toward the area of battle, requested permission to temporarily leave the formation screen to search for and recover survivors; however, the officer in tactical command (OTC) refused to grant this request. Lieutenant Green commented, "The Navy sends out many ships for just one downed pilot!! But, not one for us!"

The narrative of Cdr. Leon S. Kintberger USN, the commanding officer of the *Hoel*, is more detailed as to this aspect. Among other matters, he stated:

> Survivors of this ship were left in the water on rafts and floater nets for about forty-eight hours. During this time, fifteen men of the *Hoel* died as a result of wounds, exposure, and shock. The area in which this Task Unit was operating, and in which this vessel was sunk, was small and definitely known. The rafts were sighted and recognized by at least three groups of our planes. The air-sea rescue which works so well in picking up downed aviators *failed to function at all*. At least three officers and forty men, whom I have reported as missing in action, were seen alive in the water and on rafts [initially].
>
> It is recommended that as soon as possible after a naval engagement, that is, as soon as enemy ships have cleared the area, a thorough plan of air-sea rescue be put into effect for the saving of lives.

In the official Action Report by the senior surviving officer of the *Johnston* to COMINCH, dated 14 November 1944, via Commander Seventh Fleet, were the following comments as to the lack of prompt action to save lives:

> The 141 survivors of this ship clung to three life rafts and two floater nets for fifty hours before rescue. It is recommended that the very efficient manner in which downed *fliers* are picked up be made for rescuing *ship* survivors. This group was "zoomed" by three different friendly planes *within two hours* after the ship was sunk. *No* life rafts or food were dropped, and no help arrived for

two days and two nights. During this time, forty-five officers and men died as a result of wounds, shock and exposure. In another day without help there would have been *no* survivors of this ship.

Efforts to rescue the survivors of the *Johnston, Hoel* and *Roberts* were "put on the back burner," so to speak, but this was not the case with the loss of carriers. The Action Report filed by the *Heermann* (DD-532) of 1 November 1944 notes that when the *St. Lo* was ordered abandoned after the kamikaze attack, the OTC immediately ordered all screening vessels to pick up its survivors. After spending four hours on this mission of rescue, those screening vessels were ordered to proceed to Leyte Gulf with the men they had rescued. There were no such orders to any screening ships regarding the survivors of the *Johnston*, the *Hoel*, or the *Roberts*.

While fear of submarine and kamikaze attacks may have been the reason that not even one nearby screening vessel was sent in search of survivors of the *Johnston*, the *Hoel* and the *Roberts*, this does not seem plausible. To have every screening vessel leave the screen for four hours to rescue men from the *St. Lo*, and then take them to Leyte Gulf, exposed the carriers to such attacks. Thus, it is difficult to understand why the same, swift rescue action was not taken to find and save those who had fought valiantly until their ships were sunk.

The loss of comrades during the battle and during their long struggle in the water has had a very telling effect on the survivors. For some of them, each 25th day of October is a very difficult day; it brings back too many bad memories. One of them has told me that for years he was so emotionally overcome on that day each year, he could not get out of bed. It was and is a very painful day for many.

In this respect they have been aided in recent years through the formation of the USS *Samuel B. Roberts* Survivors Association. Meeting at reunions on that date has been helpful; it enables the survivors to have the support of one another. Some have even been involved in a larger survivors' group that encompasses men from each ship that made up Taffy 3.

Before these associations were created in recent years, the men often contacted one or more of their group, sometimes contacting families of their comrades who fell in action. Typical is the letter written on Saturday evening, 25 October 1954, by J. Dudley Moylan, former ensign, to the parents of his very close comrade in arms, John Schuman LeClercq III. It reads as follows:

Liberty in New Orleans. Left to right: Ens. Jack Barr, Peggy Wyatt, Mary Jean Johnson, Ens. John LeClercq. This was in August 1943 while Ensign LeClercq was temporarily stationed at Eighth Naval District Headquarters. Ens. Jack Barr was a fellow officer, Miss Wyatt and Miss Johnson were from Dallas and had stopped over in New Orleans en route back to Dallas from a military wedding of a friend in Florida.

Dear Mr. and Mrs. LeClercq:

I don't know whether you are as affected by anniversaries as I am. For me, each October 25th of all these years has been a troubled and agonizing time. Near nightmare in many ways, but enriching too, for I have not forgotten and am glad that I have not.

That the ship and the life aboard her went at the same time as those I loved lets my thoughts take a peculiar way. It is very easy for me to think of the *Roberts* and her men as still sailing somewhere, only I am rudely not with them. I miss them both, the living and the dead, and sometimes I can't remember in which group a friend belongs. They stay alive and stay young while I grow old. Young and carefree, young all over, young and smiling like Johnny. It is a good way to remember them.

Anyway, I have not forgotten, and, as I said, I wanted you to know that I had not.

Love,

[signed] Dud

As with other such letters from survivors to families of those killed in action, this one was treasured by the mother of John LeClercq until her death, when it then passed into the possession of her other son, Robert, who still maintains the family's file on John. In turn, one day, it will pass to Robert's first grandson, recently born, named John Schuman LeClercq IV.

The navy, in various official reports, once confidential or top-secret but now declassified, also recognized and acknowledged the valor and bravery of the men of the three destroyers and the four destroyer escorts who battled Kurita, 25 October 1944. Typical are the following comments from the endorsement of Admiral Kinkaid to the Action Report of the *Johnston*, when he forwarded it to the commander in chief, United States Fleet (COMINCH). I quote, partially paraphrasing:

The USS *JOHNSTON* together with the destroyers *HEER-MANN* and *HOEL* and the destroyer escorts *BUTLER, DEN-NIS, RAYMOND* and *SAMUEL B. ROBERTS* interposed themselves between a fast, powerful Japanese Task Force and our slow, vulnerable CVE's. By the skillful use of smoke, the launching of daring torpedo attacks, and the refusal to break off action in the face of overwhelming odds and sure losses, this intrepid little group of fighting ships accomplished one of the most heroic and gallant epics of the war. That the *JOHNSTON* [and the *HOEL* and *ROBERTS*] should have been lost were among the calculated risks of such an undertaking. [These] ships did not go down in vain; largely through [their] efforts . . . the Japanese Force was slowed down and turned back. What the Japanese had planned as an American Naval disaster was turned into a Japanese rout. The part played by [these] ships cannot be overestimated. The courageous performance of the Commanding Officer[s], officers and crew[s] . . . in the engagement off Samar Island was in keeping with the highest traditions of the naval service.

[signed] T. C. Kinkaid

To Commemorate
Each St. Crispin's Day

This day is call'd the feast of Crispian:
He that outlives this day, and comes safely home,
Will stand a tip-toe when this day is named,
And rouse him at the name of Crispian.
He that shall live this day, and see old age,
Will yearly on the vigil feast his neighbors,
And say, "Tomorow is Saint Crispian":
Then will strip his sleeve and show his scars,
 And say, "These wounds I had on Crispin's day."
Old men forget; yet all shall not be forgot,
But he'll remember with advantages
What feats he did that day: then shall our names,
Familiar in his mouth as household words,
Copeland the Captain, LeClercq and Carr,
Osborn, Smith, Serafini and Trowbridge,
Be in their flowing cups freshly remember'd.
This story shall the good man teach his son;
And Crispin Crispian shall ne'er go by,
From this day to the ending of the world,
But we in it shall be remembered;
We few, we happy few, we band of brothers;
For he today that sheds his blood with me
Shall be my brother; be he ne'er so vile,
This day shall gentle his condition:
And gentlemen in America now a-bed
Shall think themselves accursed they were not here,
And hold their manhoods cheap whiles any speaks
That fought with us upon Saint Crispin's day.

✻ ✻ ✻ ✻ ✻ ✻ ✻

With apologies to Shakespeare
King Henry V
Act IV, Scene iii.

93

In Memoriam

JOHN SCHUMAN LeCLERCQ III, Lieutenant (junior grade), United States Naval Reserve. Born 27 November 1921 at Dallas, Texas. Killed in action 25 October 1944 on board the USS *Samuel B. Roberts* (DE-413) off Samar during the Battle of Leyte Gulf, sometimes known as the Second Battle of the Philippine Sea. Secondary education: graduate of St. Mark's School of Texas (earlier known as Texas Country Day School) in Dallas, May 1939. Attended Amherst College, Amherst, Massachusetts, 1939–1941; transferred to Southern Methodist University in Dallas, receiving his B.B.A. degree in January 1943. Enlisted in U.S. Naval Reserve as an apprentice seaman 6 January 1942. Accepted appointment as midshipman, U.S. Naval Reserve on 2 April 1943, and thereupon reported to the U.S. Naval Reserve Midshipmen's School, Northwestern University, Chicago. On 1 July 1943, commissioned an ensign, and ordered to Eighth Naval District at New Orleans for temporary duty. On 14 September 1943 assigned to USS *SC-758* for temporary duty. Detached from that subchaser on 6 October 1943 and transferred to Submarine Chaser Training Center at Miami for duty under instruction. On 13 December 1943, having completed

Lt. (jg) John Schuman LeClercq,
one of the men to whose memory this book is dedicated.

that training duty, transferred to Ordnance and Gunnery School, Navy Yard, Washington, D.C. for duty under instruction. On 12 February 1944, transferred to the Naval Training Station, Norfolk, Virginia, for temporary duty in connection with the assembly and training program for destroyer escorts. Detached on 21 April 1944 and transferred to the Supervisor of Shipbuilding, United States Navy, Brown Shipbuilding Company, Houston, Texas, reporting on 24 April 1944 along with the precommissioning detail for the USS *Samuel B. Roberts*. With construction completed, that ship was commissioned 28 April 1944, at which time LeClercq reported on board. On 1 October 1944 promoted to lieutenant (junior grade) per Alnav 184. Awarded the Purple Heart and the Asiatic-Pacific Area Campaign medals, posthumously. He was the older son of John Schuman LeClercq, Jr., and Ruth Reynolds LeClercq, 5118 Live Oak Street, Dallas, Texas. He was a member of the Phi Gamma Delta fraternity, having joined at Amherst College his freshman year.

PAUL HENRY CARR, gunner's mate third class, United States Naval Reserve. Born 13 February 1924 on a farm near Webber Falls, Oklahoma. He, his eight sisters, and his parents later settled at Checotah, Oklahoma. Killed in action 25 October 1944 on board the USS *Samuel B. Roberts* (DE-413) off Samar during the Battle of Leyte Gulf, sometimes known as the Second Battle of the Philippine Sea. Graduate of Checotah High School, May 1942, where he lettered in football and baseball, and was active in the Future Farmers of America. After employment by Swift & Company for a year, he enlisted in the navy as an apprentice seaman 27 May 1943. Completing boot camp at San Diego and granted leave, he returned to Oklahoma and married Goldie Lee Jameson on 12 October 1943. They returned to San Diego, where he entered a six weeks course of instruction in the naval school for gunner's mates. Upon completion, he was promoted to gunner's mate, third class, and transferred to Norfolk as part of the precommissioning detail for the *Roberts*. He was one of the men who made the long troop train trip to Houston under Ensign LeClercq, and thus became a member of ship's company for the *Roberts* when it was commissioned on 28 April 1944. He was the only son of Thomas Henry Carr and Minnie Mae Austin Carr. He was awarded the Silver Star medal, posthumously, for conspicious gallantry and intrepidity during the battle. He was also

Paul Henry Carr, GM3c,
one of the men to whose memory this book is dedicated.

awarded the Purple Heart and the Asiatic-Pacific Area Campaign medals.

In 1985 the navy named a new guided missle frigate in his honor, the USS *Carr* (FFG-52), which was christened by Mrs. Goldie Carr Bensilhe, the widow of Paul Henry Carr, at the 1984 launching ceremony held at Todd Shipyards in Seattle. At the later ceremony in Seattle on 27 July 1985 when the *Carr* was commissioned, many former shipmates of Paul Henry Carr were in attendance, along with Mrs. Bensilhe. At the commissioning ceremony, Mr. Jack Yusen, representing the survivors of the *Roberts*, addressed the crew of the *Carr*, and his closing remarks were: "If you must fight, fight with courage, will and determination . . . we pass the legacy, the torch to you . . . sail *Carr* with pride and honor."

Born of battle, bearing a hero's name and honors, on 27 July 1985, the USS *Carr* (FFG-52) joined the fleet.

Epilogue

The ships which rescued survivors from the *Roberts*, and from the *Johnston*, the *Hoel*, and the *Gambier Bay*, consisted of two PCs and five LCIs. Not until late afternoon on 25 October were any ships organized to begin a search. According to the log book of the USS *PC-623*, the Commander Task Force 78 ordered the formation of Task Group 78.2 at 1700 and this group commenced preparations to get under way. LCDR J. A. Baxter USNR, from the state of Washington, the skipper of *PC-623* and the senior officer afloat, was placed in command of these rescue ships. The log book of the USS *LCI(R)-341* states that the rescue ships got under way at 1900, while the log book of the USS *LCI(G)-340* indicates that this group got under way at 1848. Such log book for the USS *PC-1119* says that it was under way at 1835. In any event, these slow ships were finally under way and at 0600 the next morning reached the reference point where they were to begin their search for survivors. Late that afternoon at 1640 the *PC-623* picked up a Japanese prisoner who was sitting on a floating box. He was immediately placed under guard.

At 2229 that evening, when the group was about thirty-two miles off Samar, red, green, and white flares were observed in the distance, toward Samar. Proceeding to that area, they located some survivors of the *Gambier Bay* at midnight, about eleven miles from Samar. By 0335 on 27 October this search group had recovered about 200 men from the carrier.

At 0745 other rafts were sighted. From these, one of the LCIs picked up the first men from the *Roberts*; this was the raft group containing LCDR Copeland and most of the officers. At 0837 the *PC-623* found additional rafts and from these it rescued men from the *Roberts* and *Hoel*. This constituted the final group of survivors. It was estimated that all ships involved in this search recovered about 1,150 men from the sea.

The log of the *PC-623* noted: "The survivors from the *Roberts* and the *Hoel* were oil-covered and, in addition, suffered from exposure, exhaustion, thirst, wounds and shock."

At 1019 the search group proceeded toward Leyte Gulf, arriving about fourteen hours later at 0113 on 28 October. Promptly, the rescue ships transferred all survivors to either a hospital ship or to a quarters ship.

Each survivor contacted during my research has expressed great admiration for the officers and crews of these rescue ships, and the helpful actions by each rescuer.

All of the officers and men from the *Roberts* who returned to San Francisco on the *Lurline*, and who did not require hospitalization, received thirty days' leave. After that, they were ordered to new duty stations.

LCDR **Robert W. Copeland,** the commanding officer, was born in 1910 in Tacoma, Washington. Entering the University of Washington, he enlisted in the Naval Reserve and joined its Officer Training Corps Unit. He received his degrees in business administration and law on 18 May 1935, as well as his commission as an ensign in the Naval Reserve. Admitted to the State Bar, he engaged in the practice of law at Tacoma until he entered into active duty with the navy in 1940.

During the early 1940s he advanced rapidly, and successively commanded the USS *Pawtucket* (YT-7), the USS *Black* (PYC-45), and the USS *Wyman* (De-38), before taking command of the USS *Samuel B. Roberts* in April 1944.

After returning to the United States, he attended the Naval War College, Newport, Rhode Island, until he was assigned duty at Headquarters, Fifth Naval District, Norfolk, Virginia. He was released to inactive duty on 25 January 1946, returned to Tacoma, and resumed his practice of law. Remaining an active member of the Naval Reserve, he attained the rank of rear admiral before his death on 25 August 1973. He is survived by his widow, Mrs. Harriet Copeland of Tacoma, Washington; his son, Robert W. Copeland, Jr., of Gig Harbor, Washington; and his daughter, Mrs. Suzanne Copeland Hartley of Longview, Washington.

Because of his performance in the battle off Samar, he was awarded the Navy Cross, and his citation appears in the Appendices.

Lt. **E. E. Roberts, Jr.,** the executive officer, a 1940 graduate of the Naval Academy, had a distinguished career in the navy, retiring in 1958 as a captain. After completing his thirty-day leave, he and Lt. William S. Burton, Jr., were ordered to the Bureau of Naval Personnel in Washington, D.C., to write letters of condolence to the next of kin of the men from the *Roberts* who did not survive. Lieutenant Burton was an attorney from Cleveland, Ohio, and engaged in the practice of law after the war. A graduate of Bowdoin College, he served on its Board of Trustees for many years.

Lt. **Thomas J. Stevenson, Jr.,** the communications officer, first received orders to the Sub Chaser Training Center at Miami, Florida, as an instructor. Thinking that he now had shore duty, he had his fiancee come to Florida so they could be married. By the time her slow train arrived in Miami some twenty-seven hours later, his orders had been changed to sea duty! Nevertheless, they married, and he immediately shoved off for duty in the far Pacific. En route to his new ship as the staff communications officer for a squadron of converted destroyer escorts, he was flown to Tacloban, on Leyte Island. Missing his ship, he had a few days' wait in Tacloban. Learning of a temporary cemetery at Tacloban, he located the grave of Serafini, which was marked with a crude wooden cross. The natives were busy disenterring the bodies and moving them to the new National Cemetery on Leyte Island. He reports that Serafini and several other men from the *Roberts* were reburied there. [In late August 1948 the remains of Tullio Serafini were returned to the United States and interred on 2 September in the family plot at the St. Rose Cemetery, Carbondale, Pennsylvania. The remains of those other men from the *Roberts* were removed to the National Cemetery at Manila, Philippine Islands, where they are now buried.] Discharged in 1946, Stevenson entered his family steamship business and now maintains homes in Pennsylvania and Florida. He and his wife recently celebrated their 50th wedding anniversary along with nine children and twenty grandchildren.

Ens. J. Dudley Moylan, the sonar officer, graduated from Duke University with honors, Phi Beta Kappa. Due to a serious hearing loss incurred in the battle off Samar, he was admitted to the U.S. Naval Hospital at Philadelphia. He was then assigned to duty at Miami, Florida, until the war's end. After discharge, he obtained his master's degree in English from Duke University and began a career as a professor at the University of Minnesota. Later he became a private investor and continues to reside in Minneapolis.

Ens. Jack K. Moore, the supply officer, was born at Oklahoma City on 18 October 1922. At that time his parents lived in Enid, Oklahoma, but soon moved to Salina, Kansas. Upon graduation from high school, Jack Moore entered the University of Kansas. After completing his freshman year, he joined the navy V-12 officer candidate program and was sent to the University of Pennsylvania. There, in early 1944, he was awarded a B.S. degree in economics and received his commission as an ensign in the Supply Corps of the U.S. Navy. His Supply Corps training was accomplished in the naval unit of the Wharton School of Finance at the University of Pennsylvania. It was then that he reported for duty aboard the *Roberts* at Pearl Harbor in September 1944. Upon release from active duty, he began a lifelong career with General Electric Corporation as a zone sales manager. As such he served, successively, in Bridgeport, Connecticut; Pittsburgh, Pennsylvania; Minneapolis, Minnesota; San Francisco, California; and finally, Kansas City, Missouri. There he retired in 1982, and made Leawood, Kansas, his home. He and his wife, Patricia, were married at Philadelphia in 1948; he had met her while attending the University of Pennsylvania. She died in the summer of 1995; he died on 18 October 1995. They had a son, a daughter, and five grandchildren. Jack Moore was an avid golfer all of his adult life, and played a final round with his son only a couple of days before his death.

H. Whitney Felt, a sonarman, was a senior in high school at Salt Lake City when Pearl Harbor occurred. Initially he entered the University of Utah as a pre-med student but joined the navy's V-12 officer program and transferred to the pre-med program at the University of Colorado in Boulder. There, failing the navy's mandatory swimming course, and fearing that he could never pass as a swimmer, he withdrew from the V-12 program and requested active duty.

He was sent to boot camp at Great Lakes, Illinios, where he quali-
fied as a sonarman. There his swimming instructor was very lax and
allowed him to pass. But his inability to swim would be a problem
again, even after his rescue.

At the end of his thirty days' leave, he was ordered back to
Treasure Island in San Francisco Bay to await orders to a ship. While
there, he was placed in charge of processing incoming drafts of men
from overseas. He had the power to issue a night liberty pass for
those awaiting barracks assignments.

One day a chief called from the Receiving Station and told him
that since his service record had gone down with the *Roberts*, the
navy needed to create a new one for him. Therefore, he had to pass
certain tests, including swimming, and was directed to report the
next afternoon to Yerba Buena Island for the swimming test! Felt
knew that he would fail and would be transferred from the navy to
the army. He was beside himself. The next morning, before he was
to depart for his swimming test, a young seaman with a great phy-
sique showed up at his window, awaiting reassignment. Felt asked
the young man if he could swim. Getting an affirmative answer, Felt
told him he could issue another liberty pass for him that night if he
would take the test in Felt's name. The seaman readily agreed, carried Felt's "dog tags" for identification, and took the test.

When the seaman returned, Felt inquired if he had passed the
test. The young sailor boasted that it was no problem, for he had
been on the varsity swimming team at Cornell before joining the
navy. Felt's swimming problem was solved.

But this was not the end, for a few days later another chief came
to see Felt. This chief told him that his swimming had been so remarkable, having set new records for the pool, he was to become a
member of a navy swimming team for the station at Treasure Island.
His heart sank. His ruse would be discovered; he might even be
court martialed! Fortunately, before his inability to swim was exposed, he received orders for his new duty station. Never were orders so welcome, even though he had to leave a great liberty city, San
Francisco!

After the war, Felt returned to Salt Lake City and reentered
the University of Utah. He married his high school sweetheart,
Leah Burrows, on 12 June 1947, and upon receiving his degree in
business, they moved to Oakland, California. After six years as
western regional office manager for the Burroughs Company, Felt

and his wife returned to Salt Lake City. Felt then opened a retail gift business, Felt-Buchorn. He is now semi-retired, but is very active as president of the *Roberts* Survivors Association. He and his wife, Leah, have two daughters, three sons and sixteen grandchildren, all of whom live within four miles of them.

Wayne Moses, a seaman, was born at Yale, Michigan, in 1922, and grew up on a farm with fifteen brothers and sisters. He enlisted in the navy in the Spring of 1942. After boot camp at Great Lakes, his first duty was on a supply ship taking equipment to England. Early in 1944 he was assigned to SCTC at Miami for destroyer escort training. Completing this program, he was assigned to the *Roberts*, reporting aboard at Houston, just in time for the commissioning of the ship. Since discharge from the navy, he has made his home in Ruby, Michigan.

Jack Yusen, a seaman, was born in 1926 at Elmhurst, Borough of Queens, Long Island, New York. At age seventeen he joined the navy and took his basic training at Sampson Naval Training Station, Ithaca, New York. After duty at Charleston, South Carolina, he reported aboard the *Roberts* in 1944 while the ship was in Boston. He received his discharge in June of 1946 and settled in Tulsa, Oklahoma, where he met his future wife. Then he spent forty-two years as a regional sales manager for Zep Manufacturing Company of Atlanta, Georgia. The company transferred him to Seattle in 1962, where he now resides. He and his wife have three sons.

Jack Yusen was one of the founders of the *Roberts* Survivors Association and served as its president for six years. Recently he was elected president of the Taffy 3 Association, a group made up of the survivors of all thirteen ships involved in the battle off Samar.

Vince Goodrich, a sonarman, was born at Syracuse, New York, in September 1926. He was a high school sophomore when Pearl Harbor occurred. On his seventeenth birthday in 1943 he enlisted in the navy at Syracuse, and thus did not complete his senior year of high school. After boot camp at the Sampson Naval Training Station, he was assigned to the Fleet Sound School at Key West, Florida. Upon completion of this training he was promoted to sonarman, third class. Then he was sent to Norfolk for destroyer escort training, and placed in the precommissioning detail for the *Roberts*. Accordingly, he was in the group that made the long train trip to Houston to join the ship.

Following his return on the *Lurline*, and after his thirty days' leave, which he spent in Syracuse, Goodrich reported to San Francisco for reassignment. For two weeks he was a sentry, then he received orders to the *APD-18*, an old World War I converted destroyer. After a brief stint of duty on that ship, he was transferred to San Diego for advance training at the navy's West Coast Sound School. There he helped mothball destroyers and destroyer escorts. Since Goodrich was so young and without any dependents, he was not discharged until March 1946. Requesting discharge at Long Beach, he enjoyed a brief vacation in Los Angeles. He then hitchhiked back to Syracuse and accepted a job with General Motors.

Determined to obtain an education, Vince Goodrich completed the remaining credits for high school graduation and entered Syracuse University. He continued to be active in the Naval Reserve, and as a college student was accepted into the Reserve Officer Candidate program. Upon graduation from Syracuse in the late summer of 1950, he was awarded a commission as an ensign, and at the same time, received orders to active duty in the Korean War. Now it was back to Fleet Sound School at Key West, and then to the DE-684, where he became the antisubmarine warfare officer (ASW).

In April 1953 Vince was released from active duty and returned to Syracuse, where he obtained a position in the sales division of General Motors. Then began a long career with General Motors and another company, with his final assignment at Bradford, Pennsylvania. During the interim he remained active in the Naval Reserve, attending drills at a unit located in Jamestown, New York. As a result, he attained the rank of commander USNR.

Retiring from business, Vince and his wife continue to reside in Bradford. Now he has ample time to enjoy his children and grandchildren.

James F. (Bud) Comet, a seaman, originally from West Virginia, signed up for the navy on 17 September 1943 at age eighteen. When he reported to the induction station at Logan, West Virginia, he volunteered for the navy and passed his physical, but his paperwork became fouled up. As he reached the final station, an army lieutenant congratulated him on being in the army. In shock, Bud blurted out that he had volunteered for the navy! Fortunately, a Navy lieutenant standing nearby heard this, inquired if it was true, ordered matters corrected, and sent Bud back through the lines. So Bud says that he is one of the few navy men who was actually in the army, but for only a few minutes.

After completing boot camp at Great Lakes, Comet reported to Norfolk and became part of the precommissioning detail for a new battleship, the USS *Missouri*. Once this training was completed, he received seven days' leave before his group was scheduled to be sent to Maine for the commissioning of the *Missouri*. While on leave, he lost his military I.D. card, was restricted for over a week, and thus missed going with the *Missouri* detail. As a result, he received new orders and was sent to Houston to join the crew of the *Roberts*. This time he didn't change branches of the military services; he merely obtained a new ship. He related that once he saw the *Roberts* and met its personnel, he was very happy with his assignment.

After returning on the *Lurline* and completing his thirty days' leave, Bud was assigned to the Pudget Sound Naval Ammunition Deport near Seattle. While there he met the young lady who was to become his wife, and they married on 28 February 1946. Discharged in May, Bud and his bride first went to his home in West Virginia. They soon returned to Seattle, where he obtained a job with Boeing Aircraft Company. Later he went into the service station and real estate businesses; now he works part-time with Fred Meyer, Inc. He and his wife have one son, two daughters, ten grandchildren, and, at last count, two great-grandchildren.

Richard K. Rohde, a radioman, 3rd class, was raised in New York, and finished high school in 1942 at age sixteen. He obtained a job as a page at the Guaranty Trust Company on Wall Street in New York City. In August 1943 when he became seventeen, he enlisted in the navy in New York City. After completing boot camp at Newport, Rhode Island, he was sent to the Naval Radio School at Boston. Successfully graduating from that school, he was promoted to radioman, 3rd class, and sent to Norfolk to join the pre-commissioning detail for the *Roberts*. As a result, Rohde also made that long train trip to Houston.

Rohde was one of the more seriously injured men in the battle, sustaining massive injuries to one leg. When the *PC-623* reached Leyte Gulf, he had to be placed on a stretcher for transfer to the USS *Comfort*, a navy hospital ship. It was difficult for him to walk and upon reaching the *Comfort*, he underwent surgery. The hospital ship sailed to Hollandia with Rohde and other badly wounded men from the four ships. He was transferred to the *Lurline* on a stretcher, as he still was unable to walk to any great extent. When the ship reached

San Francisco, he was first transferred to Oak Knoll Naval Hospital at Oakland California. Then began a series of transfers to various naval hospitals — at Great Lakes, Illinois; at St. Albans, New York; and, finally, the convalescent hospital at Asbury Park, New Jersey. Each transfer was by train, on a stretcher with two handlers. Fortunately, his leg was saved, but it was a real test of courage and determination for him to walk again.

After a year in the hospital, Rohde obtained a discharge, and went back to work at the Guaranty Trust Company. Then, after a brief stint at another job in New York City, he decided to further his education. Accepted at Cornell University, he obtained a degree in hotel management. After working some eighteen years as the manager of student union facilities, first at Cornell then at Ohio State, he took a position as manager of a country club in Michigan. As a result, he ended up managing three different country clubs, finally retiring in 1993 at Birmingham, Michigan, where he and his wife now live.

Because of his war injuries, Rohde decided to do volunteer work at a nearby Veterans Administration hospital. Because of his dedicated work and after only a few months as a volunteer, he is now working there three days a week as a staff employee.

Rohde married in New York City in 1947, and he and his wife have five children, eight grandchildren, and one great-grandchild.

Louis Gould was raised in Oswego, New York, where he enlisted in the navy in December 1942, immediately following Pearl Harbor. After completing boot camp at Sampson Naval Training Station, he, like Vince Goodrich, went to Fleet Sound School at Key West, graduating as a sonarman, 3rd class. He was first assigned to the USS *SC-1294* operating out of Tompkinsville, Staten Island, New York. In 1944 he was transferred to Norfolk and became part of the detail for the *Roberts*. After returning on the *Lurline* and completing his thirty-day leave, he was assigned to Shoemaker Naval Station in California for six months. He then returned to sea duty on the USS *William C. Miller* (DE-259). Discharged in February 1946, he then made his home in Virginia, where he is now retired in Petersburg.

John Macko, a fireman, 1st class, joined the navy in January 1944 in his hometown of Syracuse, New York, at age twenty-two. At the time, he was employed by Carrier Corporation, where he had completed three years of a four-year apprentice tool and die maker training program. After his thirty-day leave, following his return on the *Lurline*, he was assigned to a YR (a floating machine shop) at Long Beach, California. The YR was towed to the Philippines, where Macko remained until the war ended. Having made machinist mate, 3rd class, he was assigned to the Long Beach Naval Station, where he was discharged.

Upon discharge, Macko returned to Syracuse, completed his apprentice training program with Carrier Corporation, and worked there for twenty-eight years. Later he worked eighteen years for the Chrysler Corporation, finally retiring in Syracuse in 1988. He married Olga, in 1947, and they have two daughters and two grandchildren.

Robert M. (Mel) Harden, born in 1926, was the youngest of six boys and six girls. He grew up in the Woodberry neighborhood of Baltimore, Maryland. Being so young, he could not join the military service after Pearl Harbor as had his older brothers. When he celebrated his sixteenth birthday, he tried in vain to get his parents to let him join the navy. Finally, when he was seventeen they relented, and he enlisted and was sent to boot camp at Brainbridge in Maryland. Finishing boot camp, he was transferred to Norfolk and was assigned to the detail for the *Roberts*. It was here that he first met Ensign LeClercq, who became his division officer when they reached the *Roberts* in Houston.

After the *Lurline* and his thirty-day leave, Harden was assigned to the Sand Point Naval Air Station at Seattle, where he was discharged in April of 1947. He attended Olympic Junior College for only a few months, then went back to Baltimore, Maryland. There he worked for the American Can Company, the Army Chemical Center, and finally the U. S. Post Office. In 1982, after thirty-four years of government service, he retired. He has been a very active member of the survivors association, attending each reunion since the initial one in 1982.

Edward E. Wheaton was born in 1918 at Norwalk, Ohio, where he still lives. Due to a perfect score on his exam, his age, and his prior civilian work experience, he was enlisted as a petty officer, 2nd class. After boot camp at Great Lakes, he had ten months of schooling at the naval radio material facilities, becoming a radio technician. Once aboard the *Roberts* he was advanced to radio technician, 1st class, and was in charge of the maintenance of all radio and radar equipment on the ship.

After his thirty-day leave, Wheaton reported back to San Francisco for duty. By troop transport, he was shipped overseas to Okinawa for duty aboard the USS *Essex*, the first of three assignments to aircraft carriers. After a short tour, he was transferred to the USS *Intrepid*. On the very next day, the *Intrepid* was hit by a kamikaze plane while off Okinawa, and damaged so badly it had to limp back to the States for repairs. As the *Intrepid* began its slow journey home, he was transferred to his third carrier, the USS *Bunker Hill*. Almost immediately, it was hit by two kamikaze planes off Okinawa and had to return to the Bremerton Navy Yard at Seattle for repairs. This time he stayed aboard and returned to the States. After three months in the navy yard, the *Bunker Hill* was ready for duty, but the war suddenly ended. The ship then began ferrying troops from Pacific areas to the States. Wheaton remained on the *Bunker Hill* during its initial trip to Hawaii to bring back army troops. He says that the ship carried so many army passengers, they had to be bunked on cots located on the hangar deck.

In November 1945, Ed Wheaton received his discharge and returned to Norwalk, Ohio. He first worked at the Rockwell plant, then for Gordy's Glass Company, now for the Central Glass Company. All of the members of his immediate family have died and he now lives alone with his dog, Sheila. Still in good health, he has traveled throughout the South and West on his Harley-Davidson motorcycle. Ed is an avid sports fan — favoring, of course, the Indians and the Browns.

Kenneth W. Saunders, originally from Winston-Salem, North Carolina, received his draft notice in June 1943, the day after he graduated from high school at age eighteen. He promptly enlisted in the navy. Upon completion of boot camp at Bainbridge, Maryland, he was assigned to the naval Quartermaster School at Newport, Rhode Island. Upon graduation, he was promoted to quartermaster, 3rd class, and transferred to Norfolk to join the precommissioning detail for the *Roberts*.

Returning to the States on the *Lurline*, Saunders, like the others, received thirty days' leave which he spent in Winston-Salem. When his leave expired, he reported aboard a new seagoing tug at Miami, Florida, and sailed through the Panama Canal to the far Pacific.

Discharged in March 1946, Saunders entered Virginia Polytechnic Institute under the G.I. Bill. Receiving a bachelor of science degree in engineering, he began a lifelong career with A.T.& T. After thirty-six years he retired, and he and his wife returned to North Carolina where they now reside.

Rear Adm. **Kennosuke Torisu**, IJN, Japanese Self Defense Force, Retired. Admiral Torisu, born in 1908, graduated from the Japanese Naval Academy at Etajima in 1930. He began a distinguished career in the submarine force of the Japanese Navy until the end of WWII, rising to the rank of commander. When the United States permitted the establishment of the Japanese Self Defense Force, Admiral Torisu was recalled to active duty, ultimately retiring with the rank of rear admiral. Since the war he has written three books: *The Human Torpedo, The Study of the Japanese Navy's Failure,* and *The Study of the Conclusion of Pacific War.*

The Admiral Nimitz Museum Symposium in Kerrville, Texas, 8-9 October 1994, dealt with the Pacific Ocean campaigns which occurred during 1944. Admiral Torisu came from Japan to participate in this event, and was a presenter. His detailed paper concerned the development of the special human weapons, which we classify, generally, as the kamikaze. As he outlined, this encompassed both aerial and underwater human torpedoes. While Americans are more familiar with the Japanese use of aircraft in this respect, the concept first arose for underwater use. In early 1943 the idea for some such weapon had been suggested by a lieutenant in the submarine forces, but was shelved. Later that year a similar suggestion was broached by a lieutenant who served as a torpedo officer, as well as jointly by a lieutenant, junior grade, and an ensign, who were active in the midget submarine experiments. These last two officers suggested an actual human torpedo based on the use of their navy's most effective torpedo. They made a formal petition, written in their own blood, and submitted it to the Headquarters, Combined Fleet. This petition likewise was denied.

Admiral Torisu stated that, following the devastating American carrier aircraft attack of 17 February 1944 on the Japanese naval base at Truck Island, the high command realized that new and drastic strategic weapons were necessary. The Kamakize Corps resulted. The use of aircraft pilots in suicidal, crash-dive attacks on American ships began with the Battle of Leyte Gulf. Vice Admiral Takijiro Onishi, commander, First Air Fleet, in charge of all Japanese naval air forces in the Philippines, issued the order mobilizing such a corps immediately following the American landings at Leyte. The entry Admiral Onishi made in his personal diary, following this order, appears at the outset of this book.

The resulting damage to our ships soon became well-known to America and the world. The *St. Lo*, a Jeep carrier in Taffy 3, was an initial victim that fateful morning of 25 October 1944, off Samar. A photograph of its dramatic explosion appears elsewhere in this book.

The kamikaze planes were a dramatic new weapon. A new word entered the American vocabulary.

William F. Cordner of Riverside, Connecticut, is the only member of ship's company on the *Gambier Bay* whom I have interviewed. Born at Winnipeg, Canada, he grew up in Cranford, New Jersey. After graduating from Amherst College, he entered the Naval Reserve, and received his commission as an ensign early in 1941. After considerable naval training at Fort Schuyler, New York; the Naval Gun Factory at Washington, D.C.; the Bureau of Ordnance in the Navy Department at Washington, D.C.; Officers' Gunnery School at Jacksonville Air Base, Florida; and Bomb Disposal School, Washington, D.C.; he was then assigned to the navy's VC-10 Air Squadron in November 1943. Along with this air squadron, he reported on board the *Gambier Bay* at San Diego, California, in February 1944. A lieutenant, he was the aviation ordnance officer at the time the *Gambier Bay* and the other ships of Taffy 3 encountered Kurita's ships on 25 October 1944.

During the battle with Kurita, his station was on the flight deck of the *Gambier Bay*, supervising the loading of bombs and torpedoes on the planes. However, once the ship suffered damage to the engineering spaces and lost speed, no more planes were loaded or launched. The battle log he reconstructed on 3 November, after rescue, records that the last plane was launched at 0745. Then, he stated:

> I was on the flight deck with nothing then to do but watch and wait . . . the Japs thought we were heavy stuff and used armor piercing projecticles, most of which zoomed right through us . . . [but] about ten of which hit bulkheads and exploded. We were doomed when an early salvo hit our engine room and knocked out one of our two engines, reducing our maximum speed to eleven knots from eighteen knots. The rest [of Taffy 3], of course, continued their escape at full speed EXCEPT for the gallant destroyers and destroyer escorts which stayed back to shield us. . . . I hold

the greatest respect and admiration for the officers and crew of the *Johnston*, the *Hoel*, and the *Samuel B. Roberts*.

As Lieutenant Cordner noted, the *Gambier Bay* was doomed once the first engine room was hit by an enemy shell. When the second engine room was flooded and the ship became dead in the water, the fires generated by enemy shells became raging fires, completely out of control. His battle log entries show that at 0815 the order was given to flood all magazines; at 0830 the order was given to jettison all confidential and secret material; at 0840 the order was given to abandon ship; at 0920 the *Gambier Bay* sank.

A reproduction of the painting, "Freedom's Cost," depicting the abandonment of this carrier, appears elsewhere in this book. The original of the painting hangs in the Franklin Delano Roosevelt Presidential Library at Hyde Park, New York.

Lieutenant Cordner and his fellow officers and crewmen had much the same ordeals during their struggle to survive at sea as did the men from the *Samuel B. Roberts*. One unusual event happened to his raft group, however. He said: "During the second day in the sea, a group of natives from Samar came out and circled us in their canoes — just curious, gave us no help. . . . I guess we lost about 100-125 men in the two-day water ordeal."

Once he returned to the States on the *Lurline*, he went to his hometown, Cranford, New Jersey, to spend his thirty-day leave. While there he was interviewed by the *Cranford Journal*. A copy of that interview contains, among other matters, details regarding the survival at sea:

> It was impossible, Lt. Cordner stated, to get many life rafts into the water, and most of those were occupied by the wounded. He praised the work of the corpsmen, who swam from raft to raft, administering first aid to the wounded, and helping many of the injured onto the rafts. . . . [He and the able bodied men held onto the sides of rafts or raft nets for the 44–48 hours].
>
> The sun on the oil-covered water was so hot that he cut a piece of his pant leg to make a mask to put over his face. By the second day, many of the officers and men were losing their mental balance because of the heat and shock. He recalled that one man jumped off [a raft] and swam nearly fifty yards away. An officer went to his rescue and was attacked by sharks. Although the officer succeeded in returning the sailor to the raft, he, himself, died of loss of blood from wounds inflicted by the sharks.

After dusk of the second night, Lt. Cordner's group fired up flares. About 1:00 A.M. a patrol craft came . . . picked up some survivors . . . by 6:00 A.M. all [from his group] were safely in Leyte Gulf.

The article then relates how he and the others from the *Gambier Bay* were taken to New Guinea on LSTs, then on the *Lurline* to San Francisco.

Subsequent to the end of the war, William F. Cordner made a career as an officer with Citibank, retiring in 1983. Among other civic activities, he now serves as treasurer of the Historical Society of nearby Greenwich, Connecticut. He and his wife, Mary, have one son.

The currently living survivors of the USS *Samuel B. Roberts*, the USS *Johnston*, and the USS *Hoel* have commissioned a monument in memory of their lost comrades. Recently erected at the Fort Rosecrans National Cemetery on Point Loma in San Diego, California, the monument appropriately overlooks the Pacific Ocean. Made of birdseye granite from Georgia, it contains the names of the 525 men from the *Roberts*, the *Johnston*, and the *Hoel* who gave their lives in that battle.

Since the end of World War II, four new ships in the navy have borne names honoring the *Roberts*, its heroic commanding officer, and its heroic gunner's mate. In the 1950s, a new destroyer proudly carried the name, USS *Samuel B. Roberts* (DD-823), until decommissioned. Today, three new guided missile frigates serving in the fleet are the USS *Copeland* (FFG-25); the USS *Carr* (FFG-52); and the USS *Samuel B. Roberts* (FFG-58).

On 1 May 1991, over forty-seven years after the battle off Samar, the USS *Copeland*, operating in Philippine waters, sailed to the exact spot where the USS *Samuel B. Roberts* (DE-413) went down in its heroic battle. To commemorate that event, a memorial service was conducted on the *Copeland*. On 25 October 1994, fifty years after the battle off Samar, another special memorial service was conducted on a modern carrier, the USS *Leyte Gulf*. The navy has not forgotten, but well remembers, the gallant men of the *Roberts*, who fought so valiantly in that distant sea so many years ago and who sacrificed their lives for their country that fateful day — 25 October 1944.

The Navy Hymn

Eternal Father, Strong to Save,
Whose arm has bound the restless wave,
Who bade the mighty ocean deep
Its own appointed limits keep
Oh, hear us when we cry to thee
For those in peril on the sea.

O Trinity of love and pow'r,
Our brethren shield in danger's hour
From rock and tempest, fire and foe,
Protect them where-so-e'er they go;
Thus evermore shall rise to thee
Glad hymns and praise from land and sea.

O Lord be with us when we meet
In mem-ry of our warring Fleet,
And give us pause amid good cheer,
To honor those no longer here.
Oh, help us lift our hearts in praise
And comfort families all their days.*

* Verse 3 composed by
Rear Adm. Frank Virden USN (Ret.)

Appendices

APPENDIX A

CASUALTIES

Samuel B. Roberts Personnel Killed in Action
25 October 1944

Officers:	State
LeCLERCQ, John Schuman III, Lt.(jg)	Texas
RIEBENBAUER, Leopold P., Ens.	New York
TROWBRIDGE, Herbert W., Lt.	Massachusetts
Enlisted Personnel:	
ABAIR, Jr., Russell, S1/c	Indiana
ABRAMSON, Albert L., S2/c	New York
ANDERTON, Wilbur E., RdM3/c	North Carolina
BARD, Francis P., WT3/c	Pennsylvania
BARRETT, Harold, S2/c	Kentucky
BARTLETT, Ray E., F1/c	Michigan
BATES, Fred W., S2/c	Georgia
BINGAMAN, Richard A., F1/c	Illinois
BRADY, Norbert F., MM3/c	Massachusetts
BRAUN, Lloyd G., MM2/c	Ohio
BUTLER, Vernon R., ST3/c	Texas
BUTTERWORTH, Jr., William F., F2/c	Virginia
CADDARETTE, Jr., Joseph W., BM2/c	Ohio
CARR, Paul Henry, GM3/c	Oklahoma
CUMMINGS, Robert P., EM3/c	New York
DAVIS, John K., S2/c	North Carolina
DE BELLIS, John H., F1/c	Illinois
DECUBELLIS, Ralph, S1/c	Florida

DOWNS, Elroy, S2/c	Kentucky
FICKETT, Robert W., S2/c	Maine
FIRST, Cecil, StM1/c	Kentucky
FREYE, Albert H., MM3/c	Indiana
GALLERINI, Leonard N., MM3/c	Michigan
GOGGINS, J. C., Cox	Alabama
GOLDSTEIN, Leonard S., S2/c	Pennsylvania
GONYEA, Martin C., PhM3/c	New York
GRAY, John R., EM2/c	Texas
GREEN, Joseph F., SK2/c	New York
GREGORY, James A., S1/c	New Mexico
GROLLER, John J., GM3/c	Pennsylvania
GROVE, Frederick A., CWT	Ohio
HAAG, Justin C., MM2/c	New York
HARRIS, Woodrow W., S1/c	South Carolina
HAUSMAN, Donald R., GM3/c	Pennsylvania
HAWKINS, Hubert B., S2/c	South Carolina
HODGES, Troy T., F1/c	Missouri
HOOD, Enoch, S2/c	Florida
KENSLER, Jacob D., F1/c	Iowa
KILBURN, Fred, S1/c	Kentucky
KNISLEY, Charles E., S1/c	Maryland
KUPIDLOWSKI, Chester P., F1/c	Connecticut
KYGER, Lewis C., F2/c	Virginia
LECCI, Joseph, F1/c	New York
LEVITAN, Herman J., F1/c	New York
LOCKE, Jr., John, S1/c	South Carolina
LONGO, Louis V., F1/c	New York
MACON, Shirley R., CGM	Alabama
MAHER, Edward M., RM1/c	New York
MAZURA, Thomas J., SM1/c	Indiana
MERRITT, George H., FC3/c	Florida
MEYER, Herman E., F1/c	North Dakota
MILLER, Mike, GM2/c	Ohio
MORAN, John J., MM1/c	Pennsylvania
MORT, William C., WT3/c	Michigan
MURDE, Steve, S1/c	New York
NATTER, Charles W., SM3/c	New Jersey
NEWMILLER, John J., S2/c	Pennsylvania
O'CONNOR, Jr., Dudley B., WT2/c	New York
OLIVER, Clarence E., MM3/c	Washington, D.C.
ORLOWSKI, Joseph, S2/c	Pennsylvania
OSBORN, Jerry G., WT1/c	(?)

PAONE, John J., S2/c — Pennsylvania
PIERSON, Hilan R., CMM — West Virginia
ROSS, Charles A. S2/c — South Carolina
ROZZELLE, John T., S1/c — Alabama
SAYLOR, Jr., Arthur E., F1/c — Pennsylvania
SCHAFER, Darl H., S2/c — Pennsylvania
SCOTT, Harold K., S2/c — Delaware
SHAFFER, Russell W., S2/c — Pennsylvania
SERAFINI, Tullio J.,CRM — Pennsylvania
SMITH, Charles N., CMM — West Virginia
SPEARS, Melvin L., F1/c — Nebraska
STANSBERRY, Gilbert J., S2/c — West Virginia
STAUBACH, Charles, CEM — Ohio
STOVALL, William E., S2/c — Alabama
STREHLE, Fred A., SC1/c — California
SULLIVAN, Jr., John J., EM3/c — Massachusetts
THURMOND, Willard A., S1/c — Georgia
ULICKAS, George P., MM2/c — New York
WAGNER, Eugene, F1/c — North Dakota
WALLACE, Percy H., S1/c — Delaware
WEAVER, James K., EM2/c — Tennessee
WETHERALD, Thomas R., MM1/c — New York
WETHINGTON, Cloy W., MM2/c — California
WILSON, Charles J., S2/c — Pennsylvania
ZALESKI, Frank M., S2/c — New Jersey
ZUNAC, John R., F1/c — Pennsylvania

APPENDIX B

SURVIVORS

Samuel B. Roberts Personnel Rescued at Sea
27 October 1944

Officers:
BURTON, William S., Lt.
COPELAND, Robert W., LCDR
GURNETT, Lloyd A., Lt. (jg)
MOORE, Jack K., Ens.
MOYLAN, John Dudley, Ens.
ROBERTS, Everett E., Jr., Lt.
STEVENSON, Thomas J., Jr., Lt. (jg)
WEST, Luther A., Ens.
Enlisted Personnel:
AGUADA, Andres, CCK(AA)
ALBERT, Van J. S2/c
ALEXANDER, William C., S2/c
BISHOP, Jackson D., EM2/c
BLASZCZYK, Anthony J., CY
BLUE, Sam, S1/c
BRANDER, George N., S1/c
BRANHAN, William, S1/c
BRAY, George, S2/c
BRENNAN, Robert R., RM3/c
BRODSKY, Maurice S2/c
CANTRELL, Frank, CQM (AA)
CARBON, George B., S1/c
CATT, Frederick S., GM2/c
CAYO, Howard R., SoM2/c
CHALKLEY, John W., F1/c
CHAMBLESS, Orban "Ray," SM1/c
COLE, Cecil E., F1/c
COMET, James F. "Bud," S1/c
CONWAY, John L., COX
COOLEY, Peter, SoM3/c
COYLE, Oliver E., S1/c

CRONIN, Charles, Jr., Y2/c
DENT, Melvin H., S1/c
DOHERTY, William J., SC3/c
DOULL, Clifton E., QM3/c
DRISKILL, Edward W. "Jiggs," S2/c
DYKE, Ralph E. "Rap," TM3/c
EMANUEL, Herbert, S1/c
ESKINS, Herbert E., S1/c
FARMER, Clem J., S1/c
FELT, H. Whitney, Som3/c
FERRIS, Lin S., Bkr2/c
FIELDS, Clifford C., Bkr2/c
GENTRY, Elbert, QM2/c
GOHEEN, Chalmer J., Jr., MM2/c
GOODRICH, Vincent N., SoM3/c
GOULD, Louis A., SoM3/c
GRAVES, James S., S1/c
GRIGGS, James W., SoM3/c
HALLMAN, Curtis A., S2/c
HARDEN, Robert M. "Mel," S2/c
HARRINGTON, John E. "Red," BM1/c
HEALES, Howard A., S2/c
HELMICH, Erwin C., SC1/c
HENSLEY, Clifton G., S2/c
HERRERA, Adolph Z., S1/c
HILL, Julian L., S2/c
HINKEN, Harvey L., F1/c
HOFFMAN, Edward J., MM3/c
HOGAN, Edmund F., SC2/c
HUFFMAN, Ernest G., S1/c
HUNT, Joseph T., S1/c

INTERRANTE, Salvatore J., F1/c
JACOBS, Felix F., RdM3/c
JESTER, Marion G., S2/c
KATSUR, William, F1/c
KEDNEY, Elmer L., F1/c
KEEFE, John F., S1/c
KOUREY, Joseph, SF2/c
KILLOUGH, Archie W., S1/c
KING, Oscar M., PhM1/c
KREBS, William R., GM3/c
KROMER, Oscar C., WT3/c
KUDELCHUK, John W., F1/c
LABBE, Wilfred J. WT3/c
LANDRY, Edward P., F1/c
LENOIR, Adred C., F2/c
LIEDER, Ernest W., RM3/c
LILLARD, Neal, Jr., StM2/c
LLOYD, Jennings L., S1/c
LOBUS, William P., F2/c
LOWDER, Jake D., S2/c
LYNN, Roy W., S1/c
MACKO, John, F1/c
MARTEL, Lawrence W., F1/c
MASTERS, Royce V., SK1/c
McADAMS, S. C. "Sam," RdM3/c
McCARL, Harold R., RdM3/c
McCASKILL, Jackson R., S2/c
METZGER, Ray L., MM3/c
MORIARITY, Patrick J., F1/c
MOSES, Wayne V., S1/c
MYERS, James E., S2/c
NABORS, Joseph D., S1/c
NEIDICH, Martin, S2/c
NICHOLS, Richard G., FC3/c
O'HARA, Thomas V., S1/c
OLSON, Robert E., Bkr1/c
OOTEN, Walter S., Jr., Y3/c
PATTERSON, James E., WT3/c

PRYOR, Alvie R., MM3/c
RANDALL, Sherwood L., S2/c
RAYMUR, Charles P., RM2/c
REID, James M., S2/c
ROBERSON, James N., S1/c
ROBERTS, Jack G., S1/c
ROBERTS, Francis L., Sr., F1/c
ROBINSON, Alden F., S1/c
ROBINSON, Frank W., RdM3/c
ROHDE, Richard K., RM3/c
ROSNER, Albert, S1/c
SACOTTE, Clifford A., TM2/c
SASSARD, Robert F., S2/c
SAUNDERS, Kenneth W., QM3/c
SCHAFFER, George F., Cox
SHEPERD, Elisha, S2/c
SKAU, Rudolph H., CTM(AA)
SOKOL, William, MM2/c
STEWART, Earle E. "Pop," RdM3/c
SWIGGETT, Kenneth J., S2/c
TASE, Doyle E., S1/c
TAYLOR, Robert, S2/c
TOMLINSON, Everett L., S2/c
TUCK, Grover, S1/c
WALLACE, Cullen, CBM
WALLACE, Gene W., CY
WALSH, Robert L., FC3/c
WASHINGTON, Freddie L., StM1/c
WHEATON, Edward E., RT1/c
WIENERS, Harold G., GM3/c
WILSON, Wm. H. "Bill," S1/c
YOUNG, Donald F., S2/c
YOUNGBLOOD, Raymond J., RdM3/c
YUSEN, Jack, S2/c
ZABORSKI, Chester F., S2/c

APPENDIX C

PRESIDENTIAL UNIT CITATION

❖ ❖ ❖

THE SECRETARY OF THE NAVY

Washington

The President of the United States takes pleasure in presenting the PRESIDENTIAL UNIT CITATION to
TASK UNIT SEVENTY-SEVEN POINT FOUR POINT THREE, consisting of the USS *FANSHAW BAY* and VC-68; USS *GAMBIER BAY* and VC-10; USS *KALININ BAY* and VC-3; USS *KITKUN BAY* and VC-5; USS *SAINT LO* and VC-65; USS *WHITE PLAINS* and VC-4; USS *HOEL*, USS *JOHNSTON*, USS *HEERMANN*, USS *SAMUEL B. ROBERTS*, USS *RAYMOND*, USS *DENNIS* and USS *JOHN C. BUTLER* for service as set forth in the following

CITATION:

"For extraordinary heroism in action against powerful units of the Japanese Fleet during the Battle off Samar, Philippines, October 25, 1944. Silhouetted against the dawn as the Central Japanese Force steamed through San Bernardino Strait toward Leyte Gulf, Task Unit 77.4.3 was suddenly taken under attack by hostile cruisers on its port hand, destroyers on the starboard and battleships from the rear. Quickly laying down a heavy smoke screen, the gallant ships of the Task Unit waged battle fiercely against the superior speed and fire power of the advancing enemy, swiftly launching and rearming aircraft and violently zigzagging in protection of vessels stricken by hostile armor-piercing shells, anti-personnel projectiles and suicide bombers. With one carrier of the group sunk, others badly damaged and squadron aircraft courageously coordinating in attacks by making dry runs over the enemy Fleet as the Japanese relentlessly closed in for the kill, two of the Unit's valiant destroyers and one destroyer escort charged the battleships point-blank and, expending their last torpedoes in desperate defense of the entire group, went down under the enemy's heavy shells as a climax to two and one half hours of sustained and furious combat. The courageous determination and superb teamwork of the officers and men who fought the embarked planes and who manned the ships of Task Unit 77.4.3 were instrumental in effecting the retirement of a hostile force threatening our Leyte invasion operations and were in keeping with the highest traditions of the United States Naval Service."

> For the President
> /s/ James Forrestal
> Secretary of the Navy

APPENDIX D

Citation accompanying award of the
Navy Cross to the Commanding Officer of the
USS *SAMUEL B. ROBERTS*

✻ ✻ ✻

THE SECRETARY OF THE NAVY
Washington

The President of the United States takes pride in
Presenting the NAVY CROSS to

ROBERT WITCHER COPELAND, LIEUTENANT COMMANDER
UNITED STATES NAVAL RESERVE

for service as set forth in the following
CITATION:

"For distinguishing himself by extraordinary heroism as
Commanding Officer of a warship, the USS *Samuel B. Roberts*, (DE-413),
in a surface action with a large task force of the Japanese Fleet, off Samar,
in Philippine waters, October 25, 1944. Against an enemy force vastly superior in numbers, armament and armor, with cool deliberation he closed
to deliver a torpedo attack on heavy ships of the rapidly advancing enemy
who had taken him under fire from their large calibre guns. By this heroic
action, he thus diverted enemy fire to himself from the almost defenseless
vessels which he was protecting. Although his ship was lost in this engagement, his heroic actions were instrumental in turning back, sorely crippled,
a vastly superior enemy force. His extraordinary courage and magnificient fighting spirit in the face of terrific odds will live forever in the
memory of the officers and men who served with him that day. His conduct was in keeping with the highest traditions of the Navy of the United
States."

For the President

/s/ James Forrestal

Secretary of the Navy

*Rear Adm. Robert Witcher Copeland, who, as a lieutenant commander was
the commanding officer of the USS Samuel B. Roberts (DE-413). Because
of his extraordinary heroism as such commanding officer during
the battle off Samar, he was awarded the Navy Cross.*

APPENDIX E

Citation accompanying award of the
Silver Star, posthumously, to Paul Henry Carr
of the USS *Samuel B. Roberts*

* * *

THE SECRETARY OF THE NAVY
Washington

The President of the United States takes pride in presenting the
SILVER STAR MEDAL posthumously to

PAUL HENRY CARR, GUNNER'S MATE THIRD CLASS
UNITED STATES NAVAL RESERVE

for service as set forth in the following
CITATION:

> "For conspicuous gallantry and intrepidity as Gun Captain of a 5"/38 Mount on the USS *Samuel B. ROBERTS*, in action against enemy Japanese forces off Samar Island during the Second Battle of the Philippine Sea, October 25, 1944. With the power of the rammer lost and mechanical failures in the ammunition hoist, CARR manned his station steadfastly in the face of continuous close-range fire of enemy guns during an attack by a numerically superior Japanese surface force on the *Samuel B. Roberts*. By his outstanding technical skill and courageous initiative, CARR was instrumental in causing rapid and heavy fire from the gun to inflict damage upon an enemy heavy cruiser. Although mortally wounded by the premature detonation of a powder charge, fired by hand, CARR tried unassisted to load and ram the only projectile available to that mount after order to abandon ship had been given. His aggressive determination of duty reflect the highest credit upon CARR and the United States Naval Service. He gallantly gave his life for his country."

For the President

/s/ James Forrestal

Secretary of the Navy

APPENDIX F

Letter from Lt. (jg) Thomas J. Stevenson, Jr.,
a survivor of the *Roberts*,
to Mrs. John S. LeClercq, Jr.
written upon his arrival in San Francisco
aboard the *SS Lurline*

* * *

San Francisco 1, California
Thursday Dec. 1, 1944.

Dear Mrs. LeClercq:

I must say that I have been rather a coward about writing this letter. I tried three times yesterday to write, but I just couldn't seem to say the right things.

Mrs. LeClercq, I am going to be brutally frank and, I suppose, somewhat cruelly truthful because I think that years of fruitless hoping would be more trying to you than this one great shock.

In the morning of October 25th the *Roberts* was operating off the Phillipine Islands with a group of six escort carriers, three destroyers, and four destroyer escorts. A very superior Japanese task force consisting of battleships, cruisers and destroyers sneaked up on us under the cover of low hanging clouds. John and I went up to the bridge together to get a look at them while they were on the horizon. At that time the Jap battleships opened fire on us; they were still far outside the range of our 5" guns. John and I saw there was little chance for survival, so we shook hands and wished each other luck before going to our respective battle stations.

During the course of battle, the *Roberts* closed the range on the Japs while we laid a smoke screen to protect the carriers. Later she made a successful torpedo run on a large Jap cruiser. Up until that time we had not been hit; however, the Japanese heavy ships soon began to find our range. We were hit by many 14 inch, 8 inch, and 5 inch shells. We lost all power and the ship was dead in the water. She began to sink, and since we had expended all our ammunition, the order was given to abandon ship.

Although I had not known it during the battle, we had taken a direct hit on John's battle station. When I came out on deck to abandon ship, I looked for John's station only to find it had been completely obliterated. Everyone in the area had been killed immediately by concussion. No one suffered pain, nor were there any mangled bodies; they were all killed by a terrible blast.

John died a hero's death. He remained at his post, in one of the most exposed positions on the ship, in spite of explosions which occurred everywhere about. I spoke with him over the phones during the battle and he was as calm as any man could possibly be. He controlled the firing of the aft guns, and made great use of his 40 MM's in diverting torpedoes which were heading for the carriers. His coolness and his calm supervision were an inspiration to all the men he directed. Yes, you can rightly be proud of your son. I know I am proud to have had him as a friend.

As you probably know, John and I were much closer to each other than we were to any of the other officers; I suppose it was because we were young and enjoyed the same things. While on the ship, we developed a friendship which would have continued a lifetime; so you can imagine how it grieves me to write this letter. The only consolation I can offer is that I know that John did not suffer. We lost many men on the *Roberts*, and many of them suffered horribly in the water for two days before God blessed them with death. I thank God that John went through nothing like that.

Again, I offer my heartfelt condolences to you, his family, and to the sweet girl he loved so much, Venitia. I share with you your loss and your sorrow.

Sincerely,
/s/ Steve

(Author's notation: (1). As with others who were not saved, the navy first reported John as missing in action. This letter was received by his parents before the navy finally reported John as killed in action. (2). John's girlfriend, mentioned in this letter, was Venitia Parrott of Dallas, Texas. She later married James K. Hooper, has a family, and still resides in Dallas.)

APPENDIX G

Dedication of the
USS *Samuel B. Roberts* Memorial
Fort Rosecrans National Cemetery
San Diego, California
25 October 1995

* * *

The living survivors of the *Roberts,* the *Johnston,* and the *Hoel* raised the funds and sponsored the commissioning of a monument which lists the names of the men from these ships who were killed in the battle off Samar, 25 October 1944. With the cooperation and approval of the National Cemetery System, Department of Veteran Affairs, the Navy Department, and the Director of the Fort Rosecrans National Cemetery, this monument was erected in 1995 at a location in the Fort Rosecrans National Cemetery on Point Loma in San Diego, overlooking the Pacific Ocean and San Diego Harbor.

At 1000 hours on 25 October 1995, fifty-one years after the battle off Samar, this monument was dedicated as to the men of the *Roberts* who were killed in that engagement. This dedication occurred during a reunion of the Samuel B. Roberts Survivors' Association. There was a most impressive ceremony, attended by many naval, governmental, and civilian dignitaries. It included a U.S. Navy Band with buglers, a Color Guard, and a Firing Squad. During the ceremony, current survivors took turns reading the names of each man who was killed in that battle, with a ship's bell rung by Jack Yusen as each name was called.

In turn, John E. Harrington, former BM1c on the *Roberts,* read the words of remembrance which he had written to honor the memory of all of the ships of Task Unit 77.4.3 and the men thereof who died in that battle, viz:

YOU KNEW MY NAME
A monument stands facing the ocean overlooking a far away shore,
A polished granite pedestal listing three ships lost in a war.

YOU CALLED MY NAME
It has been fifty-one years since it happened. I know you haven't forgot.
My name has been called with the others, my death has not been for naught.

The Samuel B. Roberts Memorial, Fort Rosecrans National Cemetery, San Diego.
Sponsored by the USS Samuel B. Roberts Survivors Association.

Rear Adm. Herbert Bridge, from Seattle, is greeted by Richard K. Rohde, newly elected president of the Samuel B. Roberts Survivors Association. Admiral and Mrs. Bridge had just arrived for the dedication ceremony at Fort Rosecrans National Cemetery. 25 October 1995.

A U.S. Navy Band performs during the ceremony.

The memorial monument at Fort Rosecrans National Cemetery prior to its unveiling and dedication. This monument contains the names of each man on the USS Samuel B. Roberts, the USS Johnston and the USS Hoel who were killed in action in the battle off Samar 25 October 1944. That battle was a segment of the four-day Battle of Leyte Gulf during the initial invasion of the Philippines.

Following the ceremony, some guests continued to linger about that area of Fort Rosecrans National Cemetery and visit with each other.

YOU INSCRIBED MY NAME
My ship and my name have been listed on this granite that faces the sea,
The things that I fought and died for and shipmates who still
remember me.

YOU HONOR OUR NAMES
My family and friends stand in tribute at this spot on a far away shore.
You honor our names with your presence to be remembered for evermore.

YOU REMEMBER OUR NAMES
Though yesterday seems like a blink of the eye, fifty-one years have passed,
And etched in the eons of granite years, we know that the memories
will last.

THE THING THAT WE FEARED
We remembered "Band of Brothers," forever on watch below,
Would not be forgotten in passing of time. These are the things we know.

TO THOSE THAT FOLLOW BEHIND US
We wish you the very best.
As the years pass in remembrance, you, too, may join us in rest.

In conclusion, Mr. Harrington stated that these words and this monument demonstrate that the brave men lost in battle from such ships did
not die unknown, unloved and unnamed in performing the job which their
country had asked them to do.

The full program consisted of the following:

Master of ceremonies .... Richard K. Rohde
Welcome .... H. Whitney Felt
Invocation .... LCDR Allen, Chaplain USNR
Posting of Colors .... U.S. Navy Color Guard
Pledge of Allegiance .... Jack Yusen
National Anthem .... U.S. Navy Band
Introduction of Honored Guests .... Richard K. Rohde
Introduction of Families .... Vincent M. Goodrich
National Cemetery System .... Roger Rapp
Fort Rosecrans National Cemetery .... Helen Szumylo
Keynote Address .... CAPT Gary Erickson USNR
A Monument to Remembrance .... John E. Harrington
Reading of names of those lost
   in Action .... Survivors, with
                                     Jack Yusen, bell ringer

"America the Beautiful" ....U.S. Navy Band
Unveiling of Monument............................... Bud Comet, Dudley Moylan,
                        Bob Roberts, Ken Saunders, Tom Stevenson
Presentation of Wreath ....Peggy Carr Dodd, Rose Grove,
                Maggie Hayes, Robert LeClercq, Perry Schulze,
            Maxine Sinclair, Leotha Wells, LCDR Hugh D. Weatherl,
                family members present of men listed on the monument
"Eternal Father Strong to Save" ....U.S. Navy Band
Rifle Salute.. U.S. Navy Firing Detail
Taps .... Buglers of U.S. Navy Band
Benediction... LCDR Allen, Chaplain USNR
Retire the Colors .... U.S. Navy Color Guard
"Anchors Aweigh" ....U.S. Navy Band

Author's Note:

(1). In connection with this monument, the survivors of these three ships have raised the funds and created a perpetual endowment within the United Way of San Diego. That organization will administer such endowment, and, from its income, on the 25th of each October, hereafter, will cause an appropriate wreath to be placed beside this monument in the Fort Rosecrans National Cemetery.

(2). The survivors of the USS *Johnston* and the USS *Hoel* will conduct a similar dedication when they meet jointly in a reunion at San Diego on 25 October 1996.

(3). The survivors of the USS *Gambier Bay* and the USS *St. Lo* have raised funds for a similar monument to be erected in 1996 honoring their shipmates lost in this battle off Samar. It will be located beside the above monument to the men of the *Hoel*, the *Johnston,* and the *Samuel B. Roberts.* This monument for the *Gambier Bay* and the *St. Lo* will be dedicated by their survivors sometime during 1996.

(4). The survivors of all thirteen ships that comprised Task Unit 77.4.3 (also known by its voice radio call sign of Taffy 3), are now in the process of raising the funds for a monument to those ships and to Rear Adm. C.A.F. Sprague USN, who was their commander during the battle off Samar. It has been approved and will be erected near the old fleet landing on Harbor Drive in San Diego.

APPENDIX H

War Memorial at Amherst College
Amherst, Massachusetts

* * *

In 1946, after the conclusion of World War II, the alumni of Amherst College raised the funds for a monument and for improvements to certain athletic playing fields in memory of the sons of Amherst who lost their lives on the field of battle.

At a beautiful site on a bluff overlooking the playing fields below, with the Holyoke Range of hills in the background, this monument was installed. The area below, designated Memorial Field, includes the tennis courts, baseball diamond, and numerous fields for soccer, rugby and lacrosse.

Inscribed on top of the monument itself, in concentric circles, are the names of the former students killed in action during World War I and World War II. Among those names is John Schuman LeClercq III of the class of '43.

John LeClercq did not live to graduate from Amherst. Similar to some other students whose Amherst careers were cut short, he, too, was caught up in the maelstrom and havoc of such a great war. As the war worsened, he returned home to Dallas, joined the Naval Reserve, managed quickly to obtain a degree from Southern Methodist University, and immediately went on active duty as a naval officer.

Appropriately, this monument and its memorial field are a fitting tribute to those who so gave their lives. The inscription on the steps leading down to the monument reads:

MEMORIAL FIELD IS DEDICATED
BY THE ALUMNI
TO THE AMHERST MEN
WHO IN TWO GREAT WARS
GALLANTLY RESPONDED
TO THEIR COUNTRY'S CALL

The War Memorial at Amherst College, Amherst Massachusetts. This view is from the main campus quadrange toward the Holyoke Range. The name of John Schuman LeClercq III is one of the names inscribed thereon.

View of the War Memorial at Amherst College looking toward the quadrangle of the main campus. This memorial was erected by the alumni of the college in 1946 and contains the name of each son of Amherst killed in battle during either of the two great wars. In addition, Memorial Field below the monument area contains the playing fields for baseball, soccer, rugby, and lacrosse, as well as the tennis courts.

Undoubtedly there are many other memorials in towns across the country which list the names of the many men lost in battles. Very appropriately, the town of Checotah, Oklahoma, has established a public museum/library in honor of its son, Paul Henry Carr GM3c, who, posthumously, was awarded the Silver Star Medal for his gallant action on the *Samuel B. Roberts* off Samar.

APPENDIX I

A poem written by
Harold L. Throneburg RM3c of the USS *Dennis,*
following the conclusion of the battle off Samar

❖ ❖ ❖

The Fighting *Dennis*

The crew of the *Dennis* will never forget,
That dreadful day the enemy we met.
At dawn they struck with killing might,
On our small group they waged a fight.
Smoke was laid as our main defense,
Our crew determined and extremely tense.
Battleships and cruisers had our range,
Their destructive salvos increasingly came.
It seemed hopeless as they closed in for the kill,
Our ship was saved by maneuvering skill.
The escorts and carriers defied them all,
Although our force little, and chances small.

The seven small boys on a menacing run,
Sent devastating torpedoes into the rising sun,
And our planes with the same kind of attack,
Emptied with accuracy their torpedo rack.
For over three hours we were heavily pounded,
Our small force was practically surrounded.
Suicidal dives were made by their planes,
And one of our carriers went up in flames.
Our losses were small considering the odds,
We escaped death with the help of God.
You'll never know how cruel war can be,
Until blood and destruction you actually see,
Your shipmates killed by a bursting shell,
And wounded are living a tormenting hell.

The enemy has no respect for human life,
Willingly die for their eternal strife.
We were caught unprepared, I will have to say,
And took a beating in the worst kind of way.
But considering it all, we did a fine job,
Against Tojo and his murderous mob.
The words are not written that can fully describe,
The deathening destruction that war can imply.

Author's Note

In addition to the data in the bibliography, the following research information is provided.

Personal Interviews

With H. S. (Gus) Edwards, now deceased, of Abilene, Texas, former lieutenant USNR, who was cartographic and photographic officer on the USS *Wasatch*, the command ship for Admiral Kinkaid, commander of the Seventh Fleet; and the late Ralph N. Hooks of Abilene, Texas, former lieutenant commander USNR, who was the destroyer squadron supply officer, serving on board the USS *McCord*.

Telephone Interviews and Correspondence

With H. Whitney Felt of Salt Lake City, Utah; Vincent N. Goodrich of Bradford, Pennsylvania; Thomas J. Stevenson, Jr., of Tobyhanna, Pennsylvania; J. Dudley Moylan of Minneapolis, Minnesota; Jack Yusen of Bellevue, Washington; Jack K. Moore of Leawood, Kansas; James F. (Bud) Comet of Everett, Washington; John E. (Red) Harrington of Easton, Maryland; Mrs. Peggy Carr Dodd of Checotah, Oklahoma; Richard R. Rohde of Birmingham, Michigan; and Robert LeClercq of Wimberley, Texas.

Correspondence Only

With Edward E. Wheaton of Norwalk, Ohio; Robert M. Harden of Baltimore, Maryland; Everett E. Roberts, Jr., of Moorestown, New Jersey; John Macko of Syracuse, New York; Louis Gould of Petersburg, Virginia; Kenneth W. Sanders of Rural Hall, North Carolina; and Wayne V. Moses of Ruby, Michigan.

Official Records

The log books, war diaries, and/or action reports located in Washington, D.C., at the National Archives on Pennsylvania Avenue and the Operational Archives of the U.S. Naval Historical Center in Building 57 at the Washington Navy Yard, regarding various United States Navy ships, including: DEs *Roberts, Dennis, Raymond,* and *J.C. Butler*; DD *Heermann*; and CVEs *Fanshaw Bay, Kalinin Bay, White Plains,* and *Kitkum Bay.*

The action reports in such Operational Archives for various navy commands, including: Commander Central Philippines Attack Force (Commander SEVENTH Fleet), Serial 00302-C, dated 31 January 1945; Commander SEVENTH Fleet, Serial 000107, dated 10 January 1945; Commander Task Unit 77.4.3, Serial 00100, dated 29 October 1944; Commanding Officer of USS *Hoel* (DD-533), Serial 0050, dated 15 November 1944; Confidential Letter of senior surviving officer of USS *Johnston* (DD-557), serial 04, dated 14 November 1944, and the FOURTH Endorsement thereto by Commander SEVENTH Fleet, serial 02348, dated 3 March 1945; Commander Task Group 77.4, Serial 0098, dated 7 November 1944; Commander Task Group 77.4, Serial 00120, dated 29 October 1944; and Commanding Officer of USS *Heermann*, Serial 040, dated 1 November 1944.

Narrative Reports by Survivors

Various official narratives now located in such Operational Archives by some survivors of ships other than the *Roberts*, including: Leon S. Kintberger USN, commanding officer of the *Hoel*; Lt. Robert C. Hagen, senior surviving officer of the *Johnston*; Lt. Maurice F. Green USNR of the *Hoel*; and Lt. William S. Burton USNR of the *Roberts*.

Enemy Interrogations

Following the surrender of Japan and its occupation, the U.S. Navy conducted an interrogation of various former Japanese military officers, generally at the Meiji Building in Tokyo. These proceedings appear in several volumes, copies of which are in such Operational Archives. I reviewed a few, including these former Japanese naval officers: Vice Admiral Jisaburo Ozawa taken on 30 October 1945; Vice Admiral Takeo Kurita taken on 16 and 17 October 1944; Commander Yamaguchi, operational officer on the staff of commander in chief of 2nd Air Fleet, taken 25 October 1945; and Captain Genda, who served mainly at Imperial Headquarters in Tokyo and, finally, as commander Air Group 344 (Fighters) at war's end, taken 27 November 1945.

Official Maps and Charts

The map of the Battle of Surigao Strait which appears in this book was obtained by me from the personal files of H. S. (Gus) Edwards of Abilene. As the former cartographic officer on the command ship, *Wasatch*, he kept a copy of every map and chart made by him and his men for the Pacific invasions that occurred in 1944 in which the *Wasatch* was involved. As such officer he was intimately involved, since he and his crew created the maps for the operation orders and everything related thereto. His collection is vastly superior to the maps attached to the operation orders and action reports now located in the Operational Archives. His copies are not folded; those in the Operational Archives are folded several times and thus badly creased. In fact he had at least one map that the Operational Archives never had; so when I went to Washington, D.C. for a week of research I took with me a special copy of that map and gave it to the Operational Archives on behalf of Gus Edwards.

The track map of the Japanese Center Force and South Force was prepared for me by Rick Weatherl of Abilene, Texas, based upon data in the files of Mr. Edwards.

The reproduced map of the Battle of Leyte Gulf is printed with the kind permission of the U.S. Naval Institute.

Photographs

From Mrs. Peggy Carr Dodd of Checotah, Oklahoma, I obtained the photo of her brother, Paul Henry Carr. From Robert LeClercq of Wimberley, Texas, I obtained the two photos involving his brother, John Schuman LeClercq III, and the photo of the launching of the *Roberts* at the Brown Shipyard in Houston. From H. Whitney Felt I obtained the photo of the *Roberts* which was taken at sea from someone on the USS *W.C. Wann* (DE-412), its sister ship, just two weeks prior to the battle off Samar. Mr. Felt also supplied the photo of Rear Admiral Copeland. From National Archives II, located in College Park, Maryland, I obtained the numerous photos in this book attributed to USN/NA. The photos of the War Memorial at Amherst College were taken by the author.

Newspapers

The pages of the *New York Times* for October 1944 were used for press accounts involving the Battle of Leyte Gulf. The quote from the personal diary of Japanese Vice Admiral Takijiro Onishi, who ordered the first kamikaze attacks, is from a detailed news article in the *Houston Chronicle*, 19 November 1994, page 27A.

Magazine Articles

"We Asked For the Jap Fleet-and Got It," by Lt. Robert C. Hagen USNR, in the *Saturday Evening Post*, 26 May 1945, page 9; "The Battle as I Saw It," by Cdr. Amos Townsend Hathaway USN, in the *American Magazine*, April 1945, page 41; and "The Japs Had Us On The Ropes," by Rear Adm. C.A.F. Sprague USN, in the *American Magazine*, April 1945, page 40.

Bibliography

Only through extensive research of records in the National Archives and in the U.S. Naval Historical Center, and by contacting and interviewing former officers and crewmen who served on the *Samuel B. Roberts*, have I been able to write this story. Fortunately, a survivors association of men from that ship was organized a number of years ago. When it was created through the efforts of a few survivors, a great effort was put forth by them to locate former members of ship's company of the *Roberts*. They had great success.

The current president of that group is Mr. H. Whitney Felt of Salt Lake City, and I was able to locate him. Mr. Felt had a current list of the names and addresses of most of the living survivors and was kind enough to permit me to have a copy. Immediately I wrote a form letter to thirty-one active members requesting data. In some instances they telephoned me or I called them. That survivors association publishes a quarterly newsletter, and one issue contained an article concerning my effort to write this manuscript. This produced additional contacts.

Through months of research and correspondence, and with the active help of Mr. Felt and the survivors association, I was able to obtain recollections of many former members of ship's company for the *Roberts*. As a result, I obtained eyewitness accounts of all events from a few weeks prior to the time the commission pennant was raised for the first time to the time of the battle off Samar and the subsequent struggle of the men to survive at sea after the *Roberts* was sunk by enemy gunfire. All of this served to verify and amplify data I obtained from official records.

In addition to survivors from the *Roberts*, I also located William Francis Cordner of Riverside, Connecticut, former aviation ordnance officer on the *Gambier Bay*, and Mr. H. S. (Gus) Edwards of Abilene, Texas, former cartographic and photographic officer on the command ship, *Wasatch*. Mr. Cordner furnished significant data regarding the *Gambier Bay*, which data was most helpful, since the October log books of that carrier went to the bottom of the Philippine Sea. The maps in this book are

143

from the personal files of Mr. Edwards, and are a treasure for the researcher since they are in perfect shape.

Through Mr. Felt, I obtained a copy of an unpublished narrative entitled, *The Spirit of the Sammy-B*, by the late Robert W. Copeland, former commanding officer of the *Roberts*. It proved invaluable as a source of many details, since he was the only skipper that ship had.

From Robert LeClercq of Wimberley, Texas, the brother of Ensign John Schuman LeClercq III, I obtained some photos, letters, and the detailed recollection of former Ensign Jack Moore of Kansas, which recollection is set forth as a portion of Chapter 10. The LeClercq family has maintained a file concerning John, who was killed in the battle, and this file proved most helpful to me.

For the precise data, I reviewed the log books, war diaries, and action reports, all now declassified, of the four Jeep carriers, one destroyer, and three destroyer escorts which survived the battle off Samar, as well as the official reports of the commanding officer or senior surviving officer of the ships lost in that battle. In addition, I reviewed the action reports of the various navy flag commands affected by the battle off Samar.

To the best of my ability this story of the *Samuel B. Roberts* is accurate.

Index